A PROJECT CONTROLLER'S HANDBOOK

Insights from Twenty Years of Accounting in Project Environments

ALANA REID

 FriesenPress

One Printers Way
Altona, MB R0G 0B0
Canada

www.friesenpress.com

ISBN
978-1-03-919513-4 (Hardcover)
978-1-03-919512-7 (Paperback)
978-1-03-919514-1 (eBook)

1. BUSINESS & ECONOMICS, ACCOUNTING

Distributed to the trade by The Ingram Book Company

Our journey in life is shaped by the relationships that we establish. Everyday I am driven by my devotion to my children. However, this book would not exist without the incredible support that I received throughout my career. I would like to dedicate this effort to those that have had the greatest influence on that part of my journey:

- Ian took me on a site walk and became a most trusted friend,
- Jessica believed in me before I believed in myself, and
- Sue, my inspiration and confidante.

I also need to extend my gratitude to Gord. His assistance was deeply appreciated.

TABLE OF CONTENTS

FOREWORD

This book is going to be uncomfortable for some readers. It may even evoke anger because it challenges traditional project management roles and processes. However, it is intended to spark conversation and encourage open discussions on change.

Deepak Chopra stated that "all great changes are preceded by chaos," and the business world is experiencing this now. We face reduced workforce availability, incredible advancements in technology, and political pressures such as the increased focus on environmental, social, and governance issues. Added to these changes is a period of competition and inflation in which companies are struggling to keep their doors open. To reduce costs and offset new labour force dynamics, organizations are lowering their staffing levels and looking to technology for long-term solutions.

So why am I writing this book now, when there is already so much turmoil in business? Now is the time to engage in tough conversations. It is the time to re-invent roles and responsibilities. As the very nature of business is changing, and projects will play a critical role, now is the time to enable a collaborative team that can deliver superior results.

Historically, project managers are responsible for the scope delivery, making the day-to-day financial decisions, and preparing the associated reporting. These managers may be well versed in financial issues but could also have little knowledge in this area. Further, their time is torn between managing the delivery staff, the scope and schedule, and the budget. As governance becomes more critical, they are participating in other areas, such as the preparation of business cases and procurement support. With the increasing speed of business, volume of data, and an expanding role, the expectations on a project manager may no longer be realistic.

From a financial perspective, projects can be reminiscent of the Wild West. Accounting's involvement in this area is normally linked to investment evaluation, centralized transaction processing, and auditing. These functions are conducted at a summary level and there is a high probability of errors in detailed costing efforts. It is uncommon to have an accountant on the front lines of a project, identifying and managing issues as they arise. The inclusion of a project controller could reduce the pressure on the manager. This role could undertake the day-to-day financial activities and assist in project planning, including the preparation of business cases.

In addition, the skills for modeling and forecasting efforts are predominantly held by financial resources. It would seem logical that these individuals are developing the templates and protocols for project reporting. Maybe from a broad perspective. But centralized templates are not common. Instead, budget and reporting models are prepared in a variety of ways, frequently tailored to the individual project and manager. This approach creates inconsistency in the results. Comparative initiatives can not be measured reliably by the company if the underlying structures are not similar. Further, if organizational requirements have not been clarified, corporate inquiries are answered via ad hoc reporting. These as-needed requests add pressure on the project staff and can be subject to errors.

Does this mean that the project manager should be completely removed from the financial end of reporting? Absolutely not. These talented individuals have the detailed understanding of the tasks involved to enable successful delivery, and this experience cannot be replaced.

Their knowhow is invaluable in the estimate process, overseeing day-to-day activities, assessing schedules, and evaluating the impact of scope changes.

However, accountants are better suited to compiling this information into meaningful budget and monthly reporting packages. They are aware of other corporate considerations, including interest impacts, taxes, and human resource implications. Accountants manage internal and external financial elements on a regular basis. They work with control points and cost variances every day.

To address issues in the current business environment, accountants and project managers need to start learning from each other and working together. Egos need to be set aside, and each of the professionals involved must be willing to change. A strong, collaborative relationship between a project manager and project controller can lead to better governance. Under this structure, the manager can focus on delivery while the accountant focuses on financial reporting.

As will be demonstrated, this change in structure can also lead to improved corporate reporting and cost reductions. Even if this book does not convince you that the project controller is a vital and necessary role, you will be able to see that increased financial control and analysis can have huge impacts on costing efforts. Aside from the other benefits discussed herein, these considerations can also impact project viability. Profitability calculations, including internal rate of return, net present value, and payback period, are all dependent on the assumptions used during budgeting. These assumptions include the financial modeling approach.

This book contains the thoughts and opinions of the author, based on individual experiences. It is not intended to be a how-to guide for all aspects of project financial control. This discussion focuses on the inputs and processes used to manage project costs. It examines the relationship between control points, data, and variance explanations.

1. INTRODUCTION

I started my career in 1998, shortly after graduating from the Southern Alberta Institute of Technology. My first role was the position of Assistant Controller at a growing environmental company. The company itself was not fantastic. It had expanded rapidly through acquisitions but had failed to implement change management or control procedures. It was the Titanic. Even with no experience, I could see that it was going down. The executive team focused their efforts on raising additional funds but did not address the extensive management issues. There was little that could be done to save the company. However, its eventual bankruptcy shaped how I would view all future management opportunities. For the six months that I was working through the dissolution, I had a front-row seat to the aftermath of poor decisions. I had to console the employees who could no longer support their families, the suppliers who would never be paid, and the investors who had lost their life savings. It was devastating. Even though I did not know the concept at the time, I firmly became a believer in stakeholder value theory.

From there, I would spend the next four years in a variety of roles. I built a payroll database, worked as a government auditor, and supported start-up opportunities. Although all these experiences were interesting, nothing seemed to fit.

I vividly remember the day that would change my professional life forever. I received an unexpected call from my previous employer. He told me plainly that I was to drop everything and meet him inside of thirty minutes. Time was of the essence, and he would explain when I got there. As this was not his normal behaviour, I was intrigued, and set out to satisfy my curiosity.

That is how I found myself at a downtown penthouse suite, meeting with the managing partner of Heritage Partners Limited Partnership (HPLP). I was not there to assist with a financial problem; however, the management team quickly found out that I was studying accounting. It was not long before I was talked into assuming the role of Controller for the Deerfoot Meadows development.

At this point of my life, I had no intention of making accounting my permanent career. It was a means to an end. I was a single mother, a survivor of domestic violence, and was rebuilding my life. Accounting was the fastest route for me to put food on the table, but I was intent on pursuing an education in science. I thought that Deerfoot Meadows would be my last role as an accountant. I found financial statements and taxes plain tedious. I dreaded every minute of each workday.

Cost review for Deerfoot Meadows (March 2004)

Then, lightning struck.

The CFO for HPLP wanted me to establish the reporting and change order controls for the development. I had absolutely no experience, nor business, being in that room or challenging the various construction managers, but in I marched with all the confidence in the world. For me, it was simple. Ethics dictated that, as an accountant, I undertook the effort to understand the costs I was approving—and understand them I would. Further, I would make sure I could explain the costs to other non-construction parties. Frankly, those original managers hoped I would go away. They were not that lucky.

The tides started to change during a heated discussion regarding the costs to remove a buried garbage pile. It was an extremely expensive bill, and I was to get an abundance of documentation to support the claim from both financial and insurance perspectives. About twenty minutes into the dialogue, our project manager, Ian, ended the meeting and threw a hardhat my way. I spent the remainder of that day getting my first lessons in construction—touring the site, meeting the people, and observing the work. He spent the rest of his day getting lessons on why the financial justification mattered. These were raw and unfiltered discussions, both of us starting from defensive positions. By the end of that afternoon, Ian and I had established a starting point for our relationship. This would become one of the most collaborative and respectful working relationships of my construction career. It was the day I fell in love with projects.

Heading out for a site visit (November 2006)

Following my time with Deerfoot Meadows, I moved to a local engineering firm to support the project reporting for the East Balzac civil infrastructure development. Ron Kellam, the president of the company, noticed a change in industry trends that saw accountants exerting a greater influence over the project world. We had worked together on Deerfoot Meadows, and he asked me to become his translator, to help other accountants understand the world I had come to love. Over the five years I worked here, our team was involved with almost a hundred projects. I collaborated with the engineers, surveyors, and the external construction managers. I was taught how to read the civil engineering drawings and how to perform quantity take-offs so that I could prepare and validate estimates.

Projects like CrossIron Mills and the Bow would become Calgary area landmarks, and my involvement in them a source of life-long pride. The civil development in East Balzac would mark the start of incredible growth for Rocky View County. It was in a 2008 anniversary publication for Kellam Berg that my thoughts and approach to project accounting were first put into print. These experiences started my contemplation on process automation and predictive financial project models.

"One value-added service that has emerged is certifiable project accounting...[that] enables a client, at any point in a project, to understand where their overall project budget is...

Ulitmately the goal is to provide clients with a financial tool that will allow them to make proactive project decisions, rather than reactive."

BUSINESS IN CALGARY, MAY 2008
KELLAM BERG ENGINEERING &
SURVEYS 25TH ANNIVERSARY

It would be a tragedy that sparked my next career move. In December 2010, a good friend and colleague passed away unexpectedly. She was twenty-eight, had a contagious smile, and was looking forward to welcoming her first child. Her whole life was ahead of her. What we thought was a common cold turned out to be a rare cancer, and she was gone before we even had a chance to process what had happened. Thankfully, her daughter survived. However, this heartbreak would influence many of my future activities. Jessica always believed in me, and I felt that I had let her down. I felt bad that I was focusing on work and not enjoying my own children, when Jessica's daughter would grow up without her. Within a month of her passing, I handed in my notice with absolutely no plan.

It was at this time another incredible opportunity presented itself. With little experience in the information technology industry, I was hired to be the program controller for a large, internally developed system at an oil and gas company. Terrified at first, I soon learned that tracking labour and IT requirements was easier than contemplating the effect of erosion on dirt pile volumes. However, this type of tracking did have its own challenges. Luckily, a wonderful and supportive team surrounded me. I quickly developed a strong relationship with my supervisor, Sue. She was the first person I felt understood me, and she quickly became a source of inspiration. The beauty in the relationship was that we looked a data from opposite ends of the spectrum. She always had her eyes on the message we needed to convey, while I was happy to examine data connections from every angle to provide meaningful insights. Seemingly without words, we could communicate intent, approach, and results to produce superior reporting.

Starting the day on an ERP Project (October 2019)

That opportunity also gave me my first look at an international stage. It was a chance for me to expand my horizons beyond Alberta, beyond Canada. I was working with vendors from the United States and India on a regular basis. Ever curious, I would spend hours discussing business processes with the various representatives. I needed to learn about their methods and understand the assumptions used in building their individual budgets. I wanted to recognize the regional differences and reflect those in my forecasting techniques. This knowledge also assisted in the regular contract reviews that formed part of the payment cycle.

Since that time, I have stayed involved in both construction and information technology projects. Throughout my career, I have managed billions of dollars in delivery costs, and much more in overall returns. Although the basic reporting for the projects has not been subject to substantial change, the unique outcomes and politics of each opportunity are thrilling. Even within the same organization, project dynamics can be dramatically different. Further, as technology has rapidly improved, the methods by which the data is created, gathered, and analyzed has been an area of endless learning. Each day brings something new and exciting!

My experiences are quite different from many of my accounting peers and not part of the traditional career path. As marketing is not my strength, I have problems explaining what I do for a living. This occasionally excludes me from professional opportunities. I believe that my day-to-day activities are just part of my job. I speak in terms of system controls and data structures rather than regulations or taxes – more like an IT professional. However, I am not considered a part of this group either.

Does this difference in experience make my skills less valuable than those of my colleagues? I would argue *no*. As the importance of automation and data analytics continues to grow, I have chosen a career path that has provided the experience to manage and adapt easily to the associated changes. Further, for over twenty years I have evaluated complex opportunities, been involved in strategic planning, created process efficiencies, reduced reporting errors, enabled decisions, and identified corporate savings. These are skills held by many senior financial professionals.

Now, years after I began this journey, I will share the major lessons I have had as a project controller. The predictive elements are still emerging and will be assisted by advances in technology. The major lessons centre around communication, data control, and providing clarity on the changes the project undergoes from inception to completion.

This book is not going to discuss how to prepare a project estimate, budget, or forecast. There are fantastic sources of information on these subjects, and I encourage project professionals to use them. Organizations such as The Project Management Institute (PMI) or The Association for the Advancement of Cost Engineering (AACE) provide in-depth training on project management processes. Organizations like the Finance Modeling Institute, the Project Finance Institute, and the Corporate Finance Institute have programs to support specialized financial skill development.

Instead, this volume will focus on the practical financial aspects of project reporting. It will discuss the data relationships that exist and how to use that information to provide better, more consistent reports. We will explore how controls can be employed to support financial measurements, variance analysis, and key performance indicators (KPI). Much of the discussion will be centered on labour reporting as contract requirements have been extensively covered by existing organizations. The contents of this book will apply to individual projects and larger program initiatives, and these terms may be used interchangeably.

Although the role I have chosen has been more functional than that of my colleagues, it is no less important or strategic than other accounting positions. I hope this book reaches others in my position and lets them know they are not alone. I hope that this book sparks uncomfortable conversations, especially in a time where governance issues are critical and change is rampant.

2. WHY PROJECT ACCOUNTING MATTERS

During the review of a corporate invoicing process, I discovered that a substantial volume of projects had not been billed in months, if ever. Some of the unbilled efforts were for projects where the services had long been completed. Further, the unbilled work was not recognized in the corporate accruals.

It was the middle of December; year-end was looming over me. We had just completed a massive cost transfer between two reporting entities. I ran the usual financial reports to prepare the accrual. That is when I noticed it. There was a multi-million-dollar variance between the historic costs and those that were now being reported for the same time. No pressure at all – only a few thousand records to reconcile, correcting entries to prepare, a secondary cost load to perform, and a post-adjustment reconciliation to complete prior to year-end.

The capitalization requirements for a large, multi-jurisdictional project were not clarified during the planning stage. When reviewed, it was determined that the project assets would be owned by multiple corporate entities, depending on their final physical location. The corrective action included a full analysis of incurred and forecast costs. Additional project structures were required to support financial reporting and cost allocations. Subsequent manual adjustments, process changes, and consolidation frameworks were required.

These are real examples of costing situations that needed to be managed on the project front. Each impacted different areas of internal reporting, corporate financial statements, and key financial ratios. To be fair, not all project discrepancies are material. However, if an error is not identified, investigated, and discussed openly, the impact cannot be fully understood. In addition, the concept of materiality can be subject to interpretation at a project level. What may be considered immaterial to an organization can have huge impacts on the delivery of a project. What may not seem material at a project level could have larger company implications.

With billions spent each year on projects or service contracts, errors in the processes have real consequences for organizations and their stakeholders. It is important to get it right.

A. THE COST AND SOCIAL IMPACTS OF PROJECT ERRORS

Errors in costs at a project level affect more than just the performance of the initiative. There can be downstream effects that are not always considered. In fact, the errors may not just be one-time, standalone issues. There can be long-term consequences for the overall organizational performance. Furthermore, the application of accounting standards and tax treatments can increase the magnitude and complexity of the mistake.

An incorrect allocation between the balance sheet and income statement influences more than project costs. It will also impact net income, taxation, and shareholder returns. Imagine that vacation costs have been directly included in the construction expenses of a new asset. Besides not adhering to accounting standards, this results in an overstatement of the asset cost. As such, the value is incorrect for accounting and taxation purposes. This leads to incorrect depreciation calculations. Further, as the labour expense is understated, the resulting net income of the company is overstated. This will influence tax payments and investor returns.

It is uncomfortable, but sometimes project results are skewed in a manner that best supports team performance reviews. Is there a chance that the control structure is allowing for bonus payments to be inflated? Alternatively, are all projects managed the same? Is the company failing to consider the conditions and unique aspects of large project deliveries compared to smaller initiatives? In this case, the team could be unnecessarily penalized and subject to reduced compensation.

How is organizational overhead impacted by project errors? Are costs increasing because the internal team is spending a significant amount of time finding and correcting project inaccuracies? Have external audit costs increased due to mistakes? What pressure does this put on the financial position and operational ability of the company?

Corporate cash flows are also affected by errors in project costing. Perhaps the company is borrowing too much to fund the endeavour. This would result in higher interest costs. It would also change the company's debt to equity ratio, which in turn could affect borrowing ability. Existing covenant calculations can also be influenced by issues in project financial results. In the previous example of the billing omissions, additional investments were required to support cash outflows. Was that necessary?

Project errors also affect pricing calculations and have a social impact. In reality, no one would complain if an error reduced pricing. But what if an oversight results in inflated rates? Does it impact the consumer's ability or desire to purchase the product or service? Is undue strain being put on the end-user?

Consider the following overly simplified examples. In Figure 2-1, there is an upstream error inclusion that has been marked up three times before being passed on to the customer. The total value of the error in consumer pricing is not just the original amount, but also a compounded overage of 73 percent.

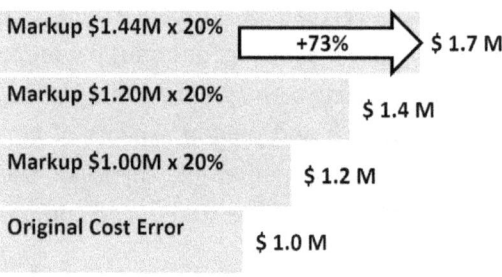

Figure 2-1: Impact of markup on project cost error

Figure 2-2 shows how this amount increases to $8.6 million if a five times multiplier is used to determine pricing. Imagine this is a simple spreadsheet error for a development of one hundred pre-sold homes. The additional price added to each house would be $86,400. As the houses are pre-sold, any cost savings to the developer during construction would not be returned to the buyers. This could go the other way, where the costs are underestimated by the same amount. The builder would be subject to the loss of out-of-pocket expenses and reduced revenues.

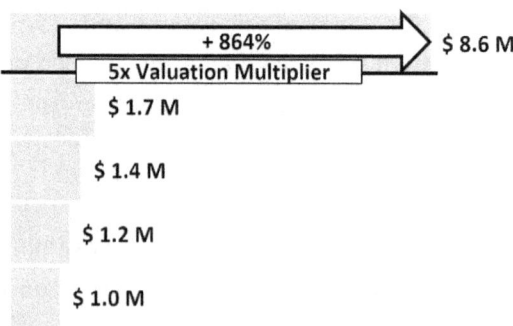

Figure 2-2: Impact of valuation multiplier on project cost error

If pricing decisions are influenced by errors and put undue pressure on the consumer, how will that affect the company's sales? Do mistakes in project costing lead to increases that damage the corporate image or competitive ability?

Figure 2-3 outlines some of the areas that are impacted when financial reporting is skewed. I encourage you to take a moment and consider how issues in projects affect each of these items, and further, how those cost anomalies interact with the other areas listed.

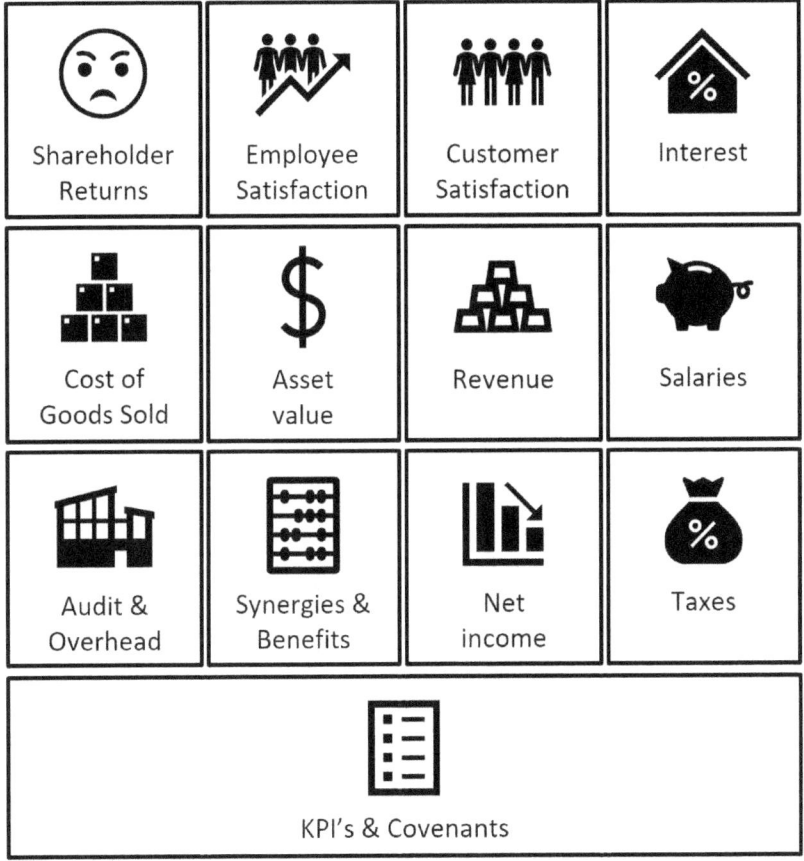

Shareholder Returns	Employee Satisfaction	Customer Satisfaction	Interest
Cost of Goods Sold	Asset value	Revenue	Salaries
Audit & Overhead	Synergies & Benefits	Net income	Taxes

KPI's & Covenants

Figure 2-3: Financial reporting areas impacted by project cost errors

B. FACTORS LEADING TO PROJECT FINANCIAL ERRORS

When I think about projects, a famous meme pops into my mind. It is a picture of two boats – a dinghy being towed by a yacht. The dinghy is named "Original Contract," and the yacht is "Change Order." Although intended as a pun, there is a certain truth in this image. It is the reality of poor project processes.

The errors that I have discovered did not happen by chance. They were revealed because I took the time and initiative to understand the larger environment of the businesses and the projects. I have spent countless hours talking to the people involved and understanding their perspective and goals. In turn, where possible, I shared the importance of the accounting and controls aspects with them. This collaboration made us all better at our jobs.

In addition to this learning, I was involved daily with the projects. Whether the activity involved a tour of the site or just a deep dive into the data, I was there ensuring a clear message could be delivered.

In my experience, there have been seven recurring project delivery issues that have led to errors in the financial reporting. These are the first items I evaluate when I walk into an unfamiliar environment. What is always surprising is that these elements are key to all aspects of business. Yet without fail, I have discovered that at least three of these delivery concerns exist in every project.

1. PROJECT STAFFING

As mentioned earlier, the manager is integral to the delivery of a project, and they tend to have considerable experience in their individual areas. However, it is also assumed that they are experts in finance, human resources, procurement, and all other areas of business that impact the project framework. Is it realistic to put this much pressure on a single resource? Many managers are not specialists in all these topics and critical requirements can be missed. Even with sufficient knowledge and supporting staff, there are limited hours in each day. The manager may not have time to properly execute their duties.

Occasionally corporate resources are assigned to the project in stewardship positions, above the manager. They are usually experts in their professions but may not be familiar with the larger business environment. In addition, there are processes that are unique within a project. If the individual does not fully understand the delivery framework and resulting organizational impacts, this could result in misunderstandings or conflicts between the management levels.

When the requirements are unclear, there may be gaps in staffing for the remainder of the project management office or delivery teams. The identified roles, along with the required skills and experience, may not be aligned with the needs of the initiative. For example, one cost reduction strategy is to use junior resources in reporting roles. This lack of experience can lead to unintentional reporting issues and additional overhead efforts to correct errors.

Staffing can also be impacted by economic conditions. When workforce availability is limited, project decisions are influenced. Resource rates may rise, which would impact the cost and viability of the undertaking. There may be limitations to the number of individuals that are available. This could result in a longer delivery schedule. If delays are not optional, the manager must hire individuals with less experience or choose to complete the initiative with reduced resourcing. How will the quality be affected by using inexperienced labour? Can existing resources deliver without burning out? If the team is put under too much pressure, retention becomes an issue. Projects will then face delays relating to transition activities.

As with any team, the right people must be in place to ensure success.

2. COMMUNICATION

The project charter is critical to communications. All parties involved need to understand the boundaries outlined in this document — scope inclusions or exclusions, costs and expected returns, and the delivery timeline. These groups include the project team, sponsors, and vendors. Scope definition is vital to strategic decision efforts and contract negotiations. Early agreement on these topics forms the basis for discussions on future changes. Information from the charter is also important to other parties. If the undertaking impacts external stakeholders, communications or advertisements need to reflect the correct messaging. If internal parties are impacted, there could be substantial adjustments to processes. Here, the involvement of change management personnel could assist the internal group in adapting to modifications in their day-to-day activities.

Information supporting subsequent changes to the scope, schedule, and costs must be clearly communicated. Each change must be defined and include how stakeholders are affected. If alternative solutions exist, the expenses and implications of these should also be identified.

It cannot be assumed that all stakeholders have detailed knowledge in the business area related to the project. The charter and change documentation should provide background for these individuals. These documents may even serve to educate decision makers. To ensure clarity, industry jargon and acronyms should be minimized. If used, these terms should be explained.

Throughout the delivery phase, there must be open communication channels between project parties. Touchpoints are used to ensure that status and issues are discussed on a regular basis. These updates must include both the positive and negative project results. If an unfavourable trend is observed, mitigation actions must be undertaken as early as possible. Failing to address these items damages the credibility of the project staff and impacts the future of the undertaking. It is also possible that a failure to act at the project level could result in substantial losses to the organization.

It is important to ensure that the right team members attend meetings and are copied on correspondence. For example, change orders routinely impact costs, so is the financial representative included in the communications? If not, why is this resource being excluded? When the accounting is managed by a central organizational group, project information must also be shared with its members. Without context, these individuals are simply compiling the numbers. The variance reporting, forecasts, and related KPIs would be a mathematical exercise. These results may not reflect information crucial to the success of the project.

Communication also means ensuring the project team has access to all information required to execute their duties. It may seem unreal, but there have been instances where contract details were withheld from financial staff. In these circumstances, the ability to correctly model or forecast for the project has been impacted. Is it enough to forward a payment schedule for modeling purposes? Are there other contract terms, such as penalties, interest, cancellation clauses, or bonuses, which should be tracked? Should these additional terms be evaluated on an as-needed basis, or does urgency impact calculation accuracy?

Of course, the key to communication is timing. Ensure discussions with the appropriate stakeholders are held in a timely manner. Conversations that are held too early or too late in the process can lead to confusion and chaos. Further, failure to communicate negative project trends could result in disaster for the organization.

3. BUDGET ERRORS

No budget is ever going to be correct; they are based on assumptions and best estimates at a single point in time. Further, inputs and designs can change drastically from the time budgeting begins until the final delivery of the project. However, gross errors occur if the planning activities are rushed or if the assumptions are incomplete.

Companies may want to define a framework for completing project-related business analyses. These investigations define the scope for many projects. Undertaking these studies without direction can result in the exclusion of key requirements. When these omissions are identified during delivery, the project will experience scope and schedule creep, which are subsequently tied to cost increases. Even with a framework in place, there is still a high probability that requirements will be missed. However, this approach could reduce the number of exceptions.

To ensure successful and consistent processes, an organization must have clear budget guidelines that are applicable to all projects. This would include information on . . .

- the templates to be used,
- the level of detail required for each submission,
- the refinement process,
- cost inclusions and exclusions,
- the budget timeline,
- project profitability measurements, and
- the approval processes.

The viability of a project is typically determined using corporate profitability measurements. Organizations will have preferred methods, such as net present value, payback period, or return on investment. Defining the budget parameters and these calculations will help in the execution of planning activities. Factors such as cost inclusions and exclusions, or the timeline, can have significant impacts on estimated returns. Complex requirements and trans-border or offshore implications require additional documentation, as they are likely to add to the expenses. It is essential to have a framework for the evaluation of these assumptions when preparing the budget.

An example of a cost that may be excluded from projects is change management. When not included in the budget, the efforts for these activities are normally captured as an overhead expense. While this strategy reduces project costs and increases the expected returns, the omission does not allow for a full evaluation of the endeavour. Overhead increases relating to a specific project will not be directly attributable to it. This approach could impact future planning and benchmarking activities.

Profitability measurements are also affected by the length of time the evaluation is completed for. Projects are undertaken for the betterment of the organization. If the endeavour is for a service or the development of physical assets for sale, these calculations may be tied to the final delivery. When long-term operations are impacted, the assessment should include a defined period outside of the project schedule. In these measurements, operational expenses are also evaluated and included as part of the estimate for returns. Considerations that would form part of these extended calculations include expenses such as maintenance fees, support costs, carrying charges, renewal obligations, and transaction fees. Further, the long-term impact may include expected savings to offset project and future overhead costs. The timing of operational effects may be outside of the project schedule and potentially not captured in estimated returns.

The process provided by the organization should also identify additional uses for budget information. Most estimates support project delivery, accounting, and audit functions, but perhaps the project needs to consider implications outside of these. Are there specific tax assumptions that need to be included? If the organization falls within a regulated industry, will the data need to be clarified and mapped to that framework?

Once the budget has been prepared, a thorough review is required. Assumptions should be compared to and verified against existing estimates. Where support is not available, the reasonability of the assumptions should be confirmed. A review of budget calculations is also required. Many errors can be attributed to simple mathematical or data entry mistakes.

When working in a project environment, it is also vital to ensure budget and presentation data is maintained. As discussed later, control point management is key to calculating and explaining variances.

4. CONTRACT PROCESSES

Contract selection is an important aspect of project management. In limited circumstances, vendors may be sole-sourced, but most contractual arrangements are subject to a tender, bid, or request for information process. Selection may also be influenced by pre-existing master agreements that limit the vendor pool.

A well-defined contracting framework can make or break a project. This process must include how updates are shared with vendors during the selection period. A bid will only be as good as the information provided to the supplier pool. They are not clairvoyant. There must be open and consistent communication during the contracting process.

The framework must also incorporate mechanisms to identify and manage outlier amounts—those that are too large or too small. What is driving the variance in the cost submissions? Are there criteria for excluding estimates with significant differences? Does the company have a history with the vendor and, if so, can it be used to evaluate potential outcomes for the current proposal? If the selection process involves vendor interviews, do not be afraid to ask questions or challenge assumptions.

Setting clear contract requirements and following defined proce-dures can also reduce future efforts for change order reporting. As mentioned earlier, this includes ensuring that the inclusions and exclusions are documented and agreed upon.

Contract payments should not simply be tied to a schedule. Ensure that there is a clear mechanism for the organization to accept third-party work and agree to payment. These could include recom-mendations from an external advisor, such as an engineer or archi-tect, confirming completion in accordance with design standards. Alternatively, this could be an internal document, endorsed by the project manager, confirming that the tasks tied to the payment have been completed.

Performance measurement criteria should also be incorporated into the framework. There needs to be a defined mechanism to hold external suppliers accountable under their contracts. Reporting on this metric involves relating the completed efforts to the financial terms of the agreement, either via a percent complete or an earned value mechanism. It is important to have the ability to determine when there is a misalignment between these components. When a project is at-risk, identified corrective actions should involve interim measurements and long-term consequences. Terms for failure to deliver often include contract termination and the identification of financial penalties.

Warranty clauses must be well defined. Again, this will involve speci-fying inclusions and exclusions. It may also require setting expecta-tions for the quality of the product and determining responsibility for the cost of repairing defects.

The relationship with a vendor may involve sharing internal data. When this situation arises, the contractual arrangement will include confidentiality requirements. The terms in the agreement must clearly identify what information can be shared, limitations to its use, data retention periods, and specific security measures or require-ments. These considerations may lead to additional clauses, includ-ing defining responsibility and penalties for compromised data.

This discussion touches on a few factors that need to be considered when selecting a supplier and entering a contract. The PMI and AACE have extensive information on contract management for those wanting to learn more about this topic.

5. INCONSISTENT PROCESSES

As organizations do not always have formal templates and processes, inconsistent reporting expectations contribute to financial discrepan-cies. Further, the impact of these miscommunications will increase as the project scope expands. Additional misunderstandings may arise if multiple locations, trans-border, or offshore work are included in the project assumptions.

Without guidance, project managers will use practices that have previously been successful for them. These will reflect their personal preferences for reporting tools, budget and forecasting approaches, and the presentation of results. However, without a standard approach, the different methodologies will impact status updates, variance analyses, and KPI metrics. This information will not be cohe-sive throughout the organization.

Think of this like a game of telephone. Without a defined framework and tools that clearly support expectations, the message will be com-municated, but not consistently. The output at the end of the line may not be exactly as desired.

To increase the reliability in communications, and comparability across initiatives, companies must define the internal project report-ing framework. What templates or tools should be used? What per-formance metrics will be employed? How will those calculations be completed? What are the project deadlines? What information should be reflected in status updates? These considerations, in addition to other elements discussed throughout this book, will only be consistent across all projects if the organization sets clear expectations.

Businesses are looking to technology to support process standardization. The use of automated platforms assists in increasing reporting accuracy and decreasing turnaround times. However, these changes cannot be made overnight, and corporate leaders need to understand implementation activities. Existing business processes must be documented. Relationships between systems must be determined. Cleansing or standardization of data may need to occur. The automation must be completed using a solid strategy. Programming rules take time to develop and, unlike manual reporting processes, cannot be changed on a whim. When companies rush these activities, the result is likely to be disappointing.

6. INCOMPLETE RISK REPORTING

Incomplete risk reporting is detrimental to project performance. Reports on risks, actions, issues, and decisions (RAID) typically include descriptions, impact evaluations, and an assignment of priority. A complete project reporting framework would include processes to manage these items. These procedures outline the . . .

- criteria for assessing impact,
- criteria for determining priority levels,
- timelines to address RAID items,
- escalation guidelines, and
- acknowledgement or sign-off requirements.

RAID items must be managed in a timely manner. Delays in decisions can impact the delivery schedule. Failure to acknowledge or mitigate risks will harm the project.

It is common to see risks identified without an associated cost-benefit calculation. Normally, this is because it can be difficult to qualify and quantify the risk. However, this exclusion limits management's ability to govern the initiative. How can a strategic decision be made if there is a lack of clarity surrounding the impacts? Even when costs are fully calculated, there could be additional factors to consider. The potential effect on contingency allowances should be acknowledged as a committed item. When the cost exceeds available funding, how will the change be paid for? Has the project forecast been evaluated to determine if there are reductions available to offset the increase? Is the organization able to allocate additional money to the project?

While most risks impact project delivery, there are some that could affect the overall viability of the company. Either way, it is important for the organization to have a clear framework in place to assess and manage RAID items.

7. TECHNOLOGY AND DATA CHALLENGES

Understanding technology and accurately managing data are big challenges in reporting. The pace of change in these areas and a resource's ability to keep up with the latest tools can affect the day-to-day processes and regular reporting activities.

The proper system access can also be an issue on the project front. It is critical to understand the entire business environment and ensure that team members can retrieve the data necessary to complete their duties. Further, project staff must understand the business policies, processes, and schedules that support the flow of information.

It is not enough to balance data from one source. If the project environment includes multiple systems, there is a potential for errors to occur between the interfaces. When these types of variances happen, they need to be identified, documented, and investigated. Problems of this nature are likely applicable to the entire organization.

This book includes discussion on some data relationships that need to be defined to clarify inputs and enable variance reporting analytics.

3. THE ROLE OF THE PROJECT CONTROLLER

A. A DIFFERENT VIEW OF PROJECTS

Projects are activities conducted within an organization. As such, the success or failure will ultimately rest on the corporate executives. These are the people that will have to respond to stakeholder questions regarding performance. Project information is shared with executives through mandatory reporting. These documents provide status updates and are used to support the company's strategic decisions. Yet frequently, critical information on project performance is not shared with this management team in a timely manner.

Many of us are familiar with the executive layer of a company. It is the group of individuals responsible for the overall health and well-being of the business. This management level is required for a company to succeed and it . . .

- provides organizational leadership,
- sets the goals to ensure success,
- delivers the structure to achieve success,
- sets financial policies, and
- enables team growth and mentorship.

One of the critical executive roles is the Chief Financial Officer. This individual assists in strategic organizational planning and is responsible for the company's financial success. They also support improvements in the financial processes and systems. Business simply could not be successful without the involvement of a highly qualified professional in this position.

What if we looked at projects like mini companies running within the organization? In Figure 3-1, each member of the project team is equated to a similar role in the executive structure. However, the role of controller is normally combined with that of the project manager. What kind of stress does this place on a project? Does the manager have the necessary skills to identify and report on critical financial issues? Are they able to remain current on accounting and project standards? Is the finance function taking critical time away from delivery? Is the governance of a project being harmed by not having a defined, mandatory controller role?

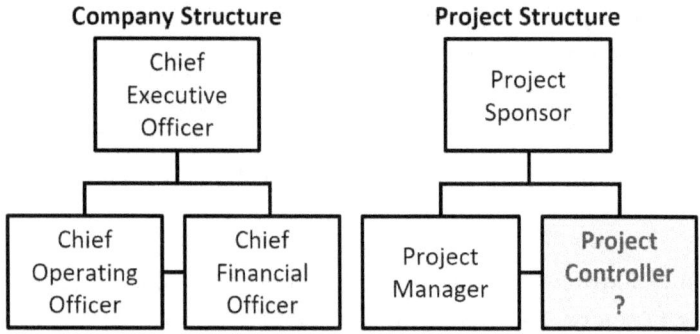

Figure 3-1: Comparison of corporate and project management organization charts

There are those that would say adding another resource to the project structure will just increase costs. This book is going to provide examples of how a controller can save time and money for both the project and organization. Further, this role does not need to be a fully dedicated resource. The finance effort should be aligned to the project's size and complexity, and one individual could report on multiple undertakings.

B. WHAT IS A PROJECT CONTROLLER?

With billions spent on projects each year, it is hard to believe the controller remains an ambiguous position, not well-defined in the professional world. I feel like this is a result of legacy processes and understanding. Historically, engineers, architects, developers, and related professionals have managed projects. These individuals are in the best position to understand the designs and delivery processes. Traditionally, the managers prepare financial reports with the support of an administrative assistant. It is rare to see an accountant in a project reporting role, and even more uncommon for them to be a senior-level resource. Periodic financial audits have been sufficient to justify project costs.

However, as the global economy expands and the volume of data increases, it is harder for one individual to effectively manage the project environment. The Project Management Office (PMO) is a group of specialized practitioners that collaborate to deliver the finished product. The increasing focus on governance may be an indicator the project controller needs to become a more prominent player.

Where is the role of a project controller defined? Neither the PMI nor AACE, leaders in project management training, have certification paths for this position. As the name implies, this role supports financial functions, so it should follow that The Chartered Professional Accountants of Canada or The American Institute of Certified Public Accountants would have programs to support the development of a project controller. Again, *no*.

Wikipedia is one of the few sources that provides a definition for the role. That definition:

> The project controller is a key member of the project team and works directly with the project manager to help define the project's goals and objectives; create and maintain a project's budget and schedule, analyze progress reported against the work schedules; and recommend actions to improve progress . . . Project controllers

are often employed by consulting firms that perform management, technology, and/or human capital work for an external client . . . [and are] responsible for over-seeing the financial health of the project by analyzing costs, revenue, risks, and pricing for the consulting firm.

The definition goes on to add that this overhead role is *normally* part of large project teams. Further, it clarifies that there are no formal qualifications required.

Project controllers are strongly associated with accounting or financial analysts. However, certain employment forums suggest that degrees in either engineering or science are essential to success. With no clear definition or certification process, requirements for this role and the associated salaries are not consistent.

Even a search for books on the topic of project controllers returns few results, with the majority of those written by non-finance professionals. This strikes me as odd. I understand that projects have traditionally been an area dominated by engineers, architects, and IT resources. However, as an accountant, I would not assume I have the skills to dictate how these professionals design and build their creations. So why, then, are the standards for project financial reporting being determined by non-finance professionals? Further, should this practice continue as expectations on corporate governance increase?

After devoting my life to this role, I have thoughts to share regarding the skills and abilities required to become a successful project controller.

- The ability to discuss and define both financial and non-financial concepts with a variety of stakeholders.
- A willingness to listen to, learn from, and work with stakeholders from diverse backgrounds.
- The ability to identify data sources and understand the relation-ships that enable reporting functions.
- A strong understanding of the policies, processes, and systems involved in supporting financial reporting.

- The ability to identify complex accounting and tax issues arising from differences in asset composition or diverse delivery locations.
- The knowledge and skills to perform data analytics in complex environments.
- The expertise to design, construct, and maintain detailed models to support all aspects of project reporting.
- The skills to present and report project results to both internal and external audiences.

This role also assists in validating that business processes are upheld, and the integrity of reporting is consistent with corporate policies and ethical requirements. The project controller ensures that records are complete and auditable. This individual may also assist in determining how different political environments and initiatives will impact project delivery.

Another benefit of having an accountant within the project structure is that they are legally bound to a code of conduct. Not all project resources are subject to these types of laws, nor do they have the associated incentives to behave in an ethical manner. While most people will act with honesty and integrity, an unregulated individual could be tempted to influence reporting for their personal gain. By the sheer nature of the profession, having an accountant involved at a project level could increase the governance of the initiative.

The role of project controller is not for all accountants. The position does require traditional accounting knowledge, but it also requires familiarity with technology environments. A person in this role must understand the supporting systems, and the relationships between them. They should be willing to question results and report parameters. A project controller should have sufficient technical abilities to work with both accounting and IT teams to resolve data issues that arise. If an accountant does not understand technology concepts and relationships, this is not the role for them.

I do believe one of the reasons the project controller role is not more predominant comes down to the impact on cost and return. I have been well paid for my services, and it has occasionally been a source of contention. However, if the controller can be viewed as a strategic business partner, there are benefits to both the project and the organization, including . . .

- Complicated financial issues can be identified during the planning phase. This reduces oversights in project assumptions and the potential for re-work during delivery.
- Incurred costs are validated at a detailed level and checked for accuracy on a regular basis. Errors are noted early, while still easy to correct, and associated overhead is kept to a minimum.
- Timely analysis of project artifacts that impact forecasting efforts. Review of these elements assists in validating cost and allocation assumptions, reducing the potential for future reporting errors and re-work.
- Forecasts are updated routinely, including cash flow and interest calculations. The organization always has the latest information available for planning purposes.

In addition to the improvements at a project level, potential organizational issues can be identified and resolved. Project financial reporting requires using multiple systems and processes. It is an area where organizational activities converge and the "silo effect" is reduced. This visibility can clarify how the systems and procedures used within a company interact.

Examples of errors that have been uncovered and managed throughout my career are discussed later in this book. These samples include process or data issues identified at both the project and company level.

C. THE CONTROLLER AND THE PROJECT MANAGEMENT OFFICE

Figure 3-2 shows two potential program structures. In the first and most common, the project controller is a part of the PMO, but is subordinate to the manager. In the second scenario, the roles are equivalent, and they work together in a collaborative fashion to deliver financial reporting.

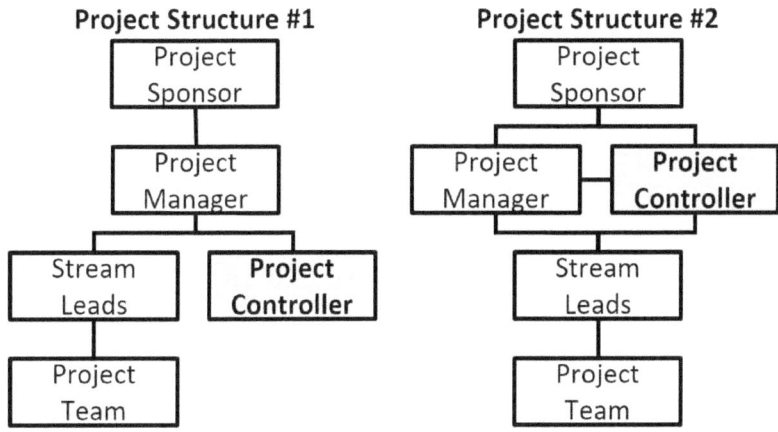

Figure 3-2: PMO structures

Although the responsibilities of the project controller do not change, the reporting structure is important. Both scenarios are functional, and the controller can still be assigned to multiple initiatives. However, the following should be considered:

- In Scenario #1, there is not a direct line between the project controller and the sponsor. As a result, the financial messaging could be manipulated prior to presentation. There are ethical considerations here, and success depends on the organization and its culture. Under this structure, program cost variance reporting could be influenced to improve performance reviews for the project management team.

- Scenario #2 works well, with a collaborative relationship between the project manager and controller. It reduces the opportunity to modify financial messaging. However, this structure can also lead to confrontation between the individuals if there is a personality issue or if there are unclear corporate reporting requirements.

Most detailed reporting frameworks are still largely determined at the project level, with formats and requirements not standardized even within an organization. The chosen management structure could influence how project performance is disclosed. Ideally, templates and processes would be determined by the company, and the reporting not subject to individual interpretations.

Sometimes, project management is outsourced to a third-party vendor. It works well in physical construction, provided the owner has final say on change orders prior to payment approval. However, it becomes more complicated and less successful in a service-based contract, such as a consulting agreement. Issues I have encountered in this type of outsourcing include . . .

- Although required to report on total project cost, the third party was unable to deliver, as the client's internal costs were not shared with the vendor.
- When preparing change orders, scope changes did not appear to be aligned with an equivalent cost change.
- Change orders for the managing vendor were approved without cost estimates, and cost was added later.
- The vendor was blamed for poor delivery by client resources, even though the vendor was not allowed to manage this workload.

When the management is outsourced, there can be a reduced visibility into the project performance. Changes may not be available or provided for review prior to approval. This can include disclosures on schedule slippage and cost overruns. When this occurs, internal project representatives may not be able to effectively perform their role. In these circumstances, any inside recommendations are completed in reaction to the external activities. These mitigation efforts could require significant effort and overhead to address.

The pros and cons of each management structure should be discussed prior to the commencement of the project. When a decision is reached, the company should implement measures to address the risks inherent in the final framework.

4. PROJECT CONTROL POINTS

Control points are a critical concept for advanced project reporting. These are events at which the assumptions are locked down and do not change. Establishing control points is key to enabling variance reporting and explanations, as differences in costs, materials, hours, and schedule will need to be evaluated.

Determining and maintaining control points has been essential through-out my career. In one situation, a large, multi-year project went over budget by about 370 percent, equating to hundreds of millions in additional spending. The financial messaging was not under my direct control, and I was not aware of the miscommunication to the project sponsors. The program was required to present regular budget revisions, but the manager chose not to report the full forecast. Presentations were not shared with me, so I was unaware the messaging was not consistent with the submitted forecast. When the variance was finally questioned, an internal audit was initiated. Because I had been tracking changes from inception and between each budget version, we were able to get through the audit process quickly. The sponsors were able to clearly identify when and how the overages occurred. The organization modified future processes so that this type of miscommunication was less likely to be repeated.

A. DEFINING CONTROL POINTS

To define control points, one needs to understand the budget timeline. Standard project management practices outline the stages of budget development. These encompass early, undefined estimates through to detailed assessments. Initial estimates are usually completed using high level assumptions and rarely support the actual delivery. As such, the corresponding risk assessment and contingency requirements are elevated. It is expected that a budget undergoes a refinement process. With each revision, assumptions are clarified, and the associated organizational risk is reduced.

As the budget becomes better defined and gets closer to approval, changes to each revision must be identified, quantified, and explained. This information includes details such as the number of resources, cost per resource, schedule, or drawing versions used. The assumptions would also encompass anticipated contract details, including expectations on the contract form (fixed rate or time and materials). If the undertaking is for an IT initiative, the RICEFW (reports, interface, conversion, enhancements, forms, and workflow) assumptions in place for each budget version would become part of the control point details. Specific accounting, regulatory, or tax assumptions used to prepare the estimates would also be fully documented.

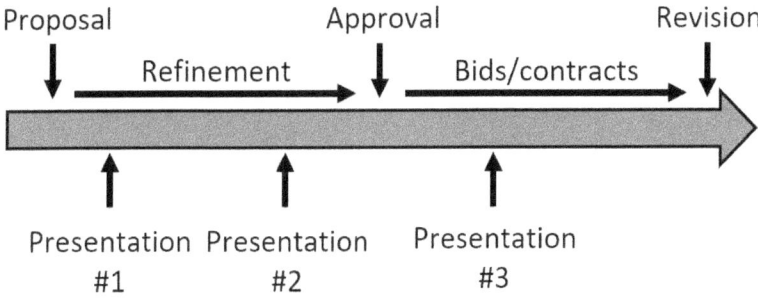

Figure 4-1: Project control points in planning phase

In addition to formal review periods, information supporting interim presentations should also be maintained as a control. It can be quite confusing when a project update is being provided and a stakeholder references an interim report that has not been considered in the revised presentation. It is even more embarrassing when the interim report backup has not been maintained and variance explanations cannot be provided. These presentation control points would not be subject to routine variance analysis, but the data should still be preserved.

After a project has been approved and is in the delivery phase, there are additional control points that need to be maintained. The most obvious are tied to the financial reporting periods. Project reporting on incurred costs should always match the periodic information in the accounting general ledger. These actual results should not change following a month-end, even if past cost elements are subsequently incurred. Current impacts of historic expenses should be accounted for in the accrual. Foreign exchange rates should also be locked down each month to match the rate in effect when the actual costs were posted. When monthly project costs are not consistent with the accounting information, managers must waste time to re-review and confirm past costing and variance explanations.

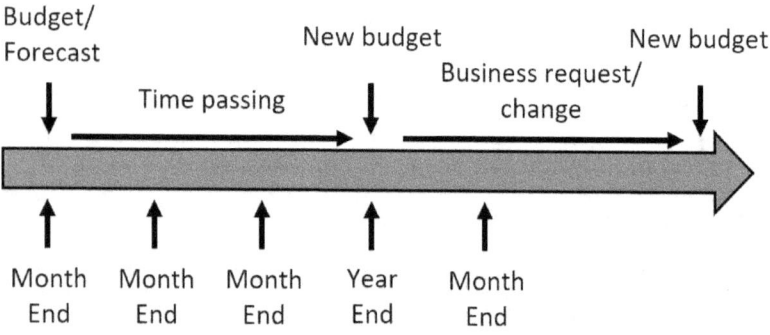

Figure 4-2: Project control points in delivery phase

In addition to the monthly reporting, there are other times at which new budgets will be required and a new control point established:

- For multi-year projects, it is common to re-baseline the costs at the end of every year. Each time this activity is completed, the resulting budget is a new control.
- Revisions are also commonly requested by organizations during times of economic change. For example, the company issues a mid-year blanket directive to reduce all costs by 20 percent.

It is important to understand the purpose and audience for each revision of the project financial information and evaluate control point requirements. At each instance, the underlying assumptions are locked and not subject to change.

B. MANAGING CONTROL POINT INFORMATION

The concept of setting and maintaining control points sounds easy and, at a high level, it is. Direct relationships are established between the cost elements from budget-to-budget, budget-to-forecast, budget-to-actual, and forecast-to-actual. Then, variances are calculated and explained as part of monthly reporting efforts.

Cost elements that need to be tracked throughout a project include . . .

- Full-time equivalent resources and/or resource headcount – Required to understand the net change in resourcing efficiency over the lifetime of a project.
- Resource hours and costs – Needed to understand how the detailed resource plan has evolved since the inception of the project.
- Design, service, or requirement amendments – Scope or material changes between the budget and the final deliverable can significantly affect cost and variance explanations.

- Schedule considerations – Changes to the timeline constitute fundamental adjustments to the deliverable and explanations.
- Contracts, including quantity changes – Understanding the cost, timing, and quantities in contracts is vital.
- Project risks – RAID items should be identified and explained to support decision-making efforts.

Change orders should be created to support formal amendments to the project assumptions and must be a part of the control documentation.

Maintaining control points becomes more difficult as the size and scope of a project grows. As the number of data points expands, it becomes harder to preserve the direct relationships between cost elements. This is particularly true in labour-intensive initiatives.

For example, take a labour role that is budgeted for full-time efforts over the duration of a three-year project. The following changes could occur for this individual role and would all need to be related back to each control point:

- The scheduled start is delayed by two months,
- The effort is reduced from full to part-time,
- The rate is changed multiple times during the project life cycle,
- The role is held by four different resources over the program duration,
- The delivery location changes dependent on the geographic location of the individual, and
- The role is budgeted for an employee but is filled by a contractor 50 percent of the time.

As one can expect, tracking this information can be difficult for even a single role. Now contemplate tracking these changes for a team comprised of a hundred unique positions scattered throughout the world.

You will note the discussion in this section encompasses cost management from the initial planning phase until the final delivery. This is also an important aspect of the reporting. The success or failure of a project is tied to its entire duration. This means costs cannot be ignored just because they are historic. In fact, these expenses may routinely impact the go-forward position and reporting, including interest calculations, asset unitization allocations, or synergy tracking.

5. PROJECT SETUP CONSIDERATIONS

A. SYSTEMS ENVIRONMENT

The project reporting environment is complex, and can involve manual and automated processes. One of the first steps in setting up the reporting is to understand the system structure. This environment will include corporate sources such as the human resource, supply chain, and accounting systems. It will also involve specific project tools and the model that will be used to prepare the overall reporting. Controllers need to determine the number of systems used and the relationships between them.

The manager and controller must work together to determine how system information will be captured and incorporated into the reporting. This includes identifying how records are transferred between the systems, as well as any gaps that may exist. Are the supporting systems fully integrated, or will additional processes be required to ensure consistency across all sources? Where there are integration issues, the alignment of the information may require data entry support or designing specific automations to enable synchronization. Each of these options will impact staffing decisions and project expenses.

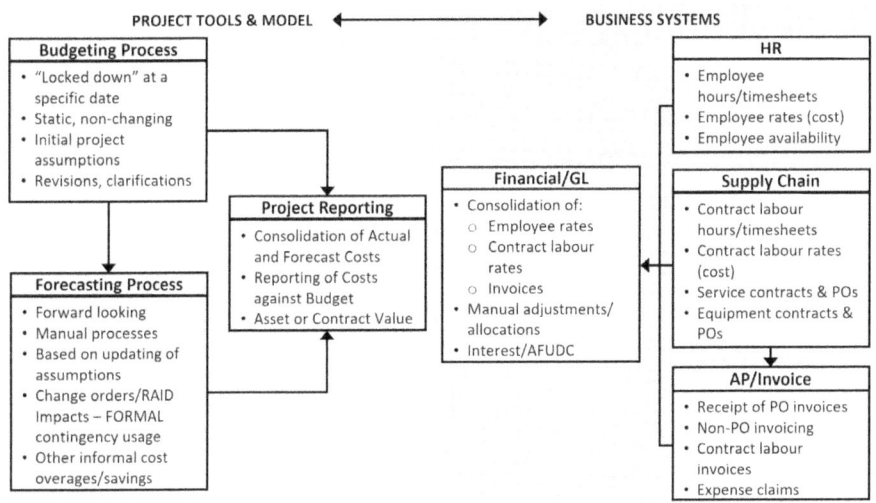

Figure 5-1: Project reporting environment

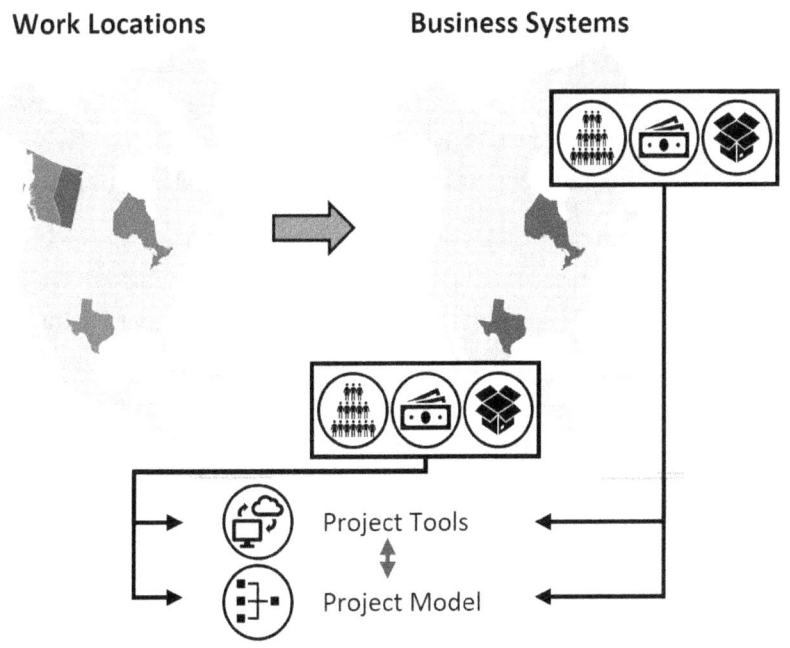

Figure 5-2: Physical work and system locations

The systems analysis should include considerations beyond the immediate structure. When the project delivery crosses borders, reporting could be impacted by the location of services or assets. In these situations, the management must determine if there are specific regional systems that need to be incorporated into the reporting structure. If the project is supporting a merger or acquisition, entirely new procedures may need to be developed to capture and consolidate data.

Having a clear picture of the systems used to support the reporting will assist with discussions on business processes and determining the project structure.

B. BUSINESS POLICIES AND PROCESSES

After gaining an understanding of the physical locations and software systems in play, it is now time to investigate the underlying business requirements. Project management must understand how an organization's policies and processes will interact with the reporting. One might ask why this is important when those activities are not owned by the project. Understanding business requirements will assist in . . .

- Determining project reporting schedules, like timesheet submission, invoice deadlines, and accrual cut-off. This knowledge can be used to develop a standard reporting calendar for the project.
- Determining the project framework. Business processes can impact the setup of a project including elements like project structures, task structure, rate determination, and capitalization or operational requirements.
- Determining the timing of transaction processing. Understanding how the systems interact and the associated processing deadlines can be used to increase the accuracy of accrual and financial estimates.

- Determining the difference between the capital and operating components of a project. Most capital project initiatives also have an operating requirement that is subject to different business processes.
- Determining management responsibilities. Organizational policies include guidelines on confidentiality, spending, and financial authorities. Understanding these policies impacts the assignment of project management duties.
- Determining reporting responsibilities. Corporate resources normally support project functions, and it is important to identify what activities the project team will undertake and how the central structure supports those efforts.

Business deadlines are used to develop a project calendar. This document is used to set clear and consistent expectations with internal and external sources. It is the basis for determining when regular touchpoints should be scheduled. The calendar will outline critical requirements for invoice or expense submissions, which affect payment schedules. Internal deadlines, such as timesheet approval and accrual submission dates, must be incorporated. Understanding these dates assists in planning staff leaves, as appropriate coverage for execution and approvals can be considered. Important update meetings with the sponsors or executives should also be included. Preparation for these meetings normally results in additional efforts, so these inclusions will assist in managing workloads. The project calendar helps establish clear expectations for all stakeholders.

Capital and operational expenses are subject to different treatments within an organization. It is important to know and understand how these functions are related and where they differ. For example, it is common for capital project labour rates to include an overhead component, while operational rates only reflect base pay allocations. How are capitalized costs reflected in departmental reporting? If standardized project rates are used, how will the variance between the capital rate and the base pay be recognized? Are there differences in the foreign exchange translation process? These understandings will play a role in variance and organizational reporting.

Business policies and processes also identify other information critical to project operations. The corporate financial authority documentation will outline the specific funding approval levels for each management role. Understanding this information allows controllers to plan how invoices and change orders are to be managed. Corporate governance documents will also provide a timeline for submitting additional funding requests. These are normally expected in advance of reaching approved budget amounts. When additional money is required, executives typically base the decision on the project's importance to strategic objectives and available corporate funds. Financial rules, such as the authority and spending limits, may be programmed into project reporting tools or accounting systems. If not, controllers must incorporate these requirements and processes into the reporting framework.

Business processes outline how information is collected and expected to flow through a company. Taking the time to understand and clarify the organizational requirements reduces miscommunications and re-work. The project controller can also use this information to prepare models that align with corporate expectations.

System procedures determine how data is captured and processed to the project. Knowing the systems environment will assist in identifying essential project controls, preparing reporting structures, and understanding how day-to-day tasks will be managed.

C. ACCOUNTING SYSTEM STRUCTURE

With an understanding of the systems environment and the business requirements, the project can now be set up for reporting purposes. Corporate accounting and project teams should work together to understand the project's needs and ensure the structure captures data appropriately. Planning this structure outside of reporting systems can highlight complexity and gaps in understanding.

The required project number(s) will be determined based on the business process requirements. The initiative should be evaluated to determine if there is a capital component, an operating component, or both. Then, the project type and number will be requested in each unique accounting system that will support the program.

For large initiatives, smaller component projects could be identified as individual tasks under a single project number. Alternatively, the organization may wish to identify each project individually and use an external mechanism to consolidate program reporting.

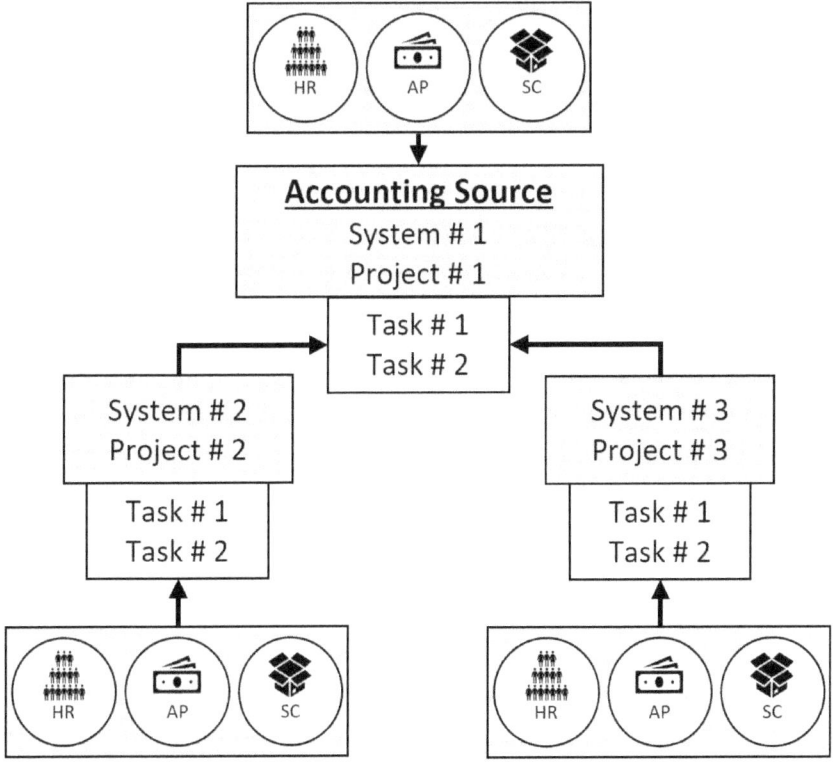

Figure 5-3: Setup of related projects in multiple systems

Next, the task structure for the project will need to be determined. Poor task structure planning can increase data entry errors. The correction of these mistakes will result in higher administrative costs.

I consistently run into project managers that want to mirror the work breakdown structure (WBS) in the accounting system. Traditional work or cost breakdown formats are functional in nature and can be complex. The data captured under these structures is important for future benchmarking efforts. However, the detailed information that is acquired has little relevance to the final cost, or unitization, of the assets.

Frequently, comprehensive formats are used to support reporting on smaller initiatives with a single deliverable. For these endeavours, the choice of task structure will not impact the unitization process. From an accounting perspective, this approach is overly complicated for these simple projects. Many of the tasks are not used and do not add value to the project reporting. However, these codes still need to be managed and reviewed. This added complexity results in unnecessary overhead expenses.

For large projects with multiple assets and delivery considerations, planning the task structure can reduce the time associated with reporting and close out activities. The following paragraphs will discuss an alternate approach to organizing these complex projects.

In large projects, is it easier to create a single task for each asset to be unitized than to create a full WBS? An asset task could be used to track the labour and materials directly associated with its development. Cost types would be managed using the financial expense categories. Under this approach, all direct expenditures are attributed to the asset throughout the delivery schedule. When the project is over, reconciliation is minimized. The subsequent allocation efforts are limited to shared expenses or overhead amounts, such as management costs and interest. Not all projects result in the construction of an asset, but the same concept could apply to service initiatives. For example, the task structure for an IT delivery project could be simplified to reflect specific releases or sprints.

Human nature is another consideration for large project task structure development. Some resources may not understand the purpose of an overly complicated breakdown. These individuals tend to take the easiest path and will use a single reporting code for timesheet purposes. As a result, any benefits of a defined WBS structure will be lost. Also, the opportunity for time to be allocated incorrectly increases as the structure expands. Overhead efforts to validate and correct time increase in proportion, and these efforts add cost to the project.

Sample Work Breakdown		Sample Cost Breakdown		Sample Asset Breakdown	
Description	*Task #*	*Description*	*Task #*	*Description*	*Task #*
Contracts	**1.0**	**Administration**	**1.0**	Prototype (Asset # 1)	1.0
Prepare bid documents	1.1	Project planning	1.1	Final (Asset # 2)	2.0
Bid submission date	1.2	Project management	1.2	Project Management	3.0
Bid review	1.3	Travel & expense	1.3		
Award contract	1.4	**Research & Development**	**2.0**		
Procurement	**2.0**	Sketches	2.1		
Order materials	2.1	Mockup	2.2		
Order equipment	2.2	**Manufacturing**	**3.0**		
Hire staff	2.3	Prototype	3.1		
Construction	**3.0**	Mockup	3.2		
Preparation	3.1	Final	3.3		
Start	3.2	Production drawings	3.3.1		
Phase 1	3.3	System	3.3.2		
Activity #1	3.3.1				
Activity #2	3.3.2				

Figure 5-4: Comparison of common task structures

For larger initiatives, the best answer should be determined through consultation between project and accounting staff. It is likely that both sides will need to compromise.

Where possible, simplify the reporting structure, keeping only necessary codes. If feasible, assign individuals to specific task codes, so that reporting requirements cannot be confused. If there are multiple systems in play, maintain naming conventions across systems.

Minimizing the project task structure will reduce the opportunity for errors and simplify approval processes.

D. REPORTING STRUCTURE

Another consideration for setup is the reporting structure used to track contract and project costs.

If the project is for a single contract, the structure may be an individual file used to track progress, or it could be a report generated from a contract management system. If the project requires the consolidation of several contracts, the reporting structure is likely to contain multiple files to support cost tracking.

Figure 5-5 shows a simple project consolidation structure. In this example, there are multiple vendors, each with their own reporting model. For Vendor #1, these reports are further broken down to support each unique contract. This layout also includes three individual labour teams. Using this approach, results can be discussed with individual delivery managers while respecting privacy considerations. The team level reporting is then combined into a consolidated project labour overview.

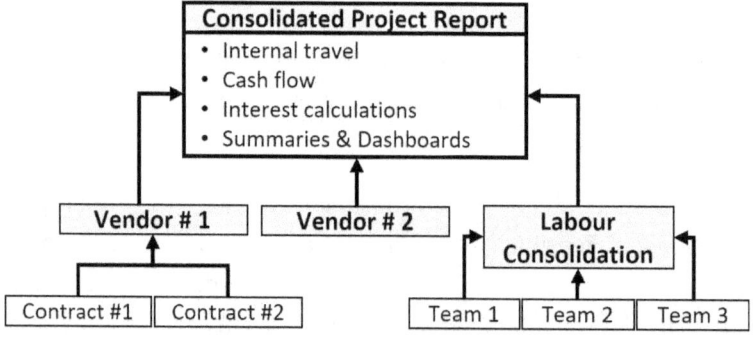

Figure 5-5: Consolidated project reporting structure

All individual modules are compiled into an overall project report. This document captures all costs and uses the information to create a cash flow estimate. The cash flow is subsequently used to calculate project interest charges, if applicable. The consolidation also contains the summaries and dashboards required for presentations.

Within each supporting workbook, it is necessary to determine the type of information that needs to be captured. Parameters that require clarification include . . .

- What is the frequency of reporting?
- What level of detail is required for each reporting segment?
- How are changes to the budget going to be captured?
- What level of commentary is required?
- What contract considerations need to be tracked?

These detailed pieces should break the project components into meaningful and manageable segments. The reporting setup must respect any internal and external confidentiality requirements.

Each supporting module should contain summaries and dashboards. These will assist with focusing conversations with vendors and internal managers during reviews.

It is important to mention that technology solutions, such as Power BI, can be used to assist in creating reporting modules. These approaches help to establish standard views across the company, reducing efforts at the project level. However, when automation is employed, audit requirements must be considered. From an accounting perspective, each period should have a clear cut-off and data should not change after that point. If the solution is tied to a live source, the periodic reports may not constitute an auditable record. These automations should include a process for reconciling between the periodic reporting and the live information.

E. REVIEW POINTS

The responsibility for delivering the project on time and within budget still rests with the manager. The project controller is responsible for compiling the financial data and consolidating it into meaningful reports. The parties need to discuss these results on a regular basis.

The timing for routine cost conversations should also be part of the setup process. These touchpoints are used to . . .

- confirm or update forecast assumptions,
- confirm approved cost changes have been captured appropriately,
- confirm incurred costs,
- discuss outstanding issues or actions,
- review results, variances, and KPIs, and
- discuss risk management scenarios as applicable.

The question remains: how often should these routine reviews be conducted?

If a project has been budgeted on a weekly basis, does it follow that weekly reviews are required? I would argue that detailed weekly reviews are not efficient and only add unnecessary overhead to projects. I suggest that this structure lends itself more to the justification of staffing levels rather than to project health.

Financial meetings take focus and time away from the project delivery. The time spent in the weekly meeting is better spent progressing the project. The discussions are normally around run rate costs—particularly related to timesheet information. As covered later in this book, timesheets can be validated without needing to meet. With respect to invoiced costs, the processing of these items to the accounting general ledger is not a weekly event. As the project manager would be reviewing and approving the invoices prior to posting, this adds to the redundancy of weekly meetings.

To accommodate accounting processes, regular touchpoints must occur at least once a month. This would exclude change order and RAID meetings, which may need to be held more frequently depending on the complexity of the project.

It becomes the project manager's responsibility to ensure the controller is copied on communications that will impact project costs or schedules. This would include new hire or termination information. It could relate to contract or travel approvals. Normally, the project controller would be an integral part of the change process, including attending meetings on change orders or RAID evaluations. If an emergency arises, the controller could ensure that financial assumptions are accurately documented, and assessments are not delayed.

In most cases, the monthly review is sufficient. The requirements for these should be clear, and the meeting should follow a schedule. These meetings are most efficient when held as part of the monthly accrual process. This timing will assist in ensuring the total value reflects the latest project assumptions. It allows for any cost corrections to be submitted prior to month-end. Further, it ensures the forecast aligns with the project manager's expectations.

It is the project controller's responsibility to ensure changes to assumptions are incorporated into the forecast. The controller must also update incurred cost data. Report information should be provided to the project manager in advance of the meeting, allowing time to review and digest the impacts of the updates.

The meetings should be relevant to the size and complexity of the initiative. It is unnecessary to have lengthy discussions for small projects with few changes, particularly if reports are provided in advance. In these circumstances, a sign-off from the project manager may be an acceptable substitute for a formal meeting. Project staff must consider the most effective use of time when scheduling touchpoints.

Attendees should also be considered when planning meetings. Critical resources must be present, but the routine inclusion of secondary staff is not required. These additional individuals are not normally active participants in the meeting. Their time is better spent on delivery items. Instead, the appropriate supervisor should coordinate and manage any required follow-up activities. Secondary staff members would be invited to participate in meetings when their knowledge provides clarity or insight into a specific issue.

The framework for interim cost evaluations is a corporate decision. However, I challenge organizations to look at the real benefits of weekly reviews. Is a weekly process worth the time taken from project delivery or potential cost overruns?

The considerations in this chapter only reflect requirements for a healthy project. If the project delivery is at risk, additional meetings may be required so that concerns can be addressed, and mitigation actions planned.

F. PROJECT CLOSURE CONSIDERATIONS

The controller also needs to work with corporate accounting to determine requirements for successful project closure. These assumptions should be discussed in the planning stage to clarify the effect on budgeting efforts.

Items that will need to be verified include . . .

- Are there any associated retirements when the new asset is delivered?
- What is the value of the asset retirement?
- How will staff be transitioned back to their original duties and service locations?
- Are there any cross-company billing requirements or valuation issues?
- How will final third-party invoicing be managed?

- What is the process for recognizing contractual obligations extending outside the project schedule?
- What group will be responsible for the final project reporting and reconciliations?
- What is the framework for tracking and reporting long-term project benefits or synergies?
- Who is responsible for the long-term organizational tracking?

These considerations could impact discussions pertaining to the project's viability. Post-closure assumptions relating to the above may increase the operational cost estimates for the project. They impact staffing requirements and schedules in the periods after delivery, including transitional planning. These expenses would need to be captured in the budget and forecast assumptions.

6. LABOUR REPORTING OVERVIEW

Labour reporting requires significant efforts and is, in my experience, one of the most inconsistent and incorrectly managed aspects of project reporting. It involves tracking resource data through multiple systems and then consolidating that information into meaningful project reports.

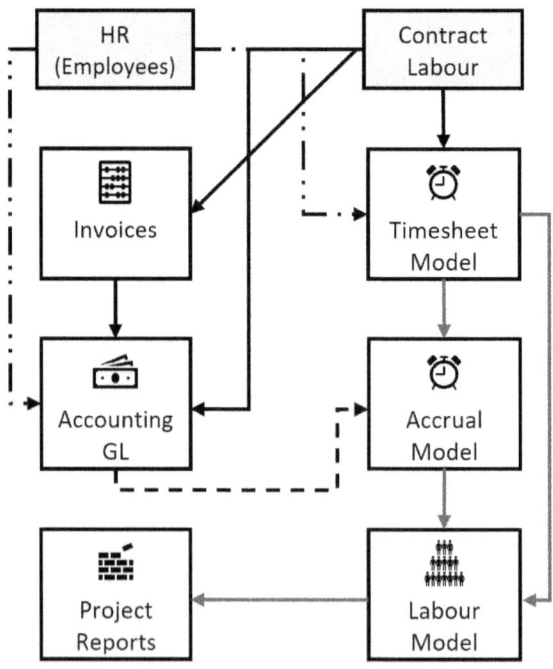

Figure 6-1: Overview of labour reporting data flow

A. WHAT IS LABOUR REPORTING?

Labour is a complex area and is governed by different forms of legislation. In addition to the legal complications, the complexity of labour reporting increases as the size of a project expands and delivery locations are added. As team size grows, so does the number of hours required to properly support its management.

Labour reporting is more than timesheets, and it is more than just reporting the actual costs being charged to the initiative. At every stage of the project, the controller supports the labour budget and forecasting activities as well as the human resource (HR) management. Further, this person constantly reviews the time and costs for completeness and correct allocation. Then, the variances are identified, and the project team works together to manage impacts to the cost or schedule as a result.

Project Setup	• Position planning with HR • Location requirement planning • Asset requirement planning	• Determining team structure and timesheet coding requirements • Security/access planning
Weekly Activities	**Monthly Activities**	**Other Activities**

• Project Controller
  ▪ Prepare timesheet report
  ▪ Follow up on exceptions
• Delivery Leads
  ▪ Review & approve stream timesheets
  ▪ Note exceptions
• Project Manager
  ▪ Approve project timesheet report
  ▪ Provide support for exception follow up, as required
	• Delivery Managers
	  ▪ Review & update stream forecast assumptions
	  ▪ Approve stream accrual/month end actuals
	• Project Controller
	  ▪ Support forecast updates
	  ▪ Prepare exception reporting
	  ▪ Prepare & submit accrual
	  ▪ Report actuals
	• Project Manager
	  ▪ Approve project accrual/month end actuals
	  ▪ Provide support for exception follow up, as required
		• Quarterly/Annual duties as directed by organization
		  ▪ Typically, these mirror month end reporting activities
		• Year end may involve new budgeting activity for continuation of project
		• Annual labour reconciliations (hours and cost)
		• Annual position planning with Human Resources
		• Audit support
		• On and off-boarding support

Project Closeout	• Return of corporate assets • Removing security access	• Support resource return to pre-project positions • Termination activities

Figure 6-2: Overview of labour reporting activities

Figure 6-2 provides a listing of activities supported throughout the project lifecycle. This book is going to focus on the finer points of the recurring reporting—timesheets, budgets, forecasts, variances—but it is important to note that actions exist in all project stages.

B. WHY IS LABOUR REPORTING SO PROBLEMATIC?

Communication is a key component of overseeing a labour-intensive project. It is important the delivery leads, manager, and controller work as a coordinated team to reduce errors in project setup. Simple miscommunications regarding the use of a single planned position can take hours to resolve. Controllers need to ensure both the delivery and project managers clearly understand their team composition. Using the regular touchpoints to review current forecasts against budgeted positions can lead to huge overhead cost savings.

Confidentiality related to employee records can restrict the project team's ability to prepare accurate reports. The information can be hard to obtain, and if access is granted, there are normally limitations on how the details can be shared within the project reporting structure. For example, I have been involved in scenarios where, as the controller, I had access to names and pay rates but could not share the information with the manager. It was exceedingly difficult to have a conversation with the person responsible for the delivery and budget. In another example, I could not share data with a non-resident manager, even though this individual was responsible for the budget.

Labour reporting requires a fundamental understanding of human-resource-related issues, including topics such as payroll, overhead, taxation, and work visas. When planning a project team, these items must be taken into consideration, and setup must involve consultation with the HR group.

Team size can impact reporting efforts. For projects supported using manual spreadsheet processes, large teams and long schedules can impact workbook speed and stability. Labour efforts must be reported in their entirety, meaning that prior, current, and future team members all require forecasting and tracking. As imagined, reporting on only this aspect for large teams can consume a great deal of time. Supporting models can become extremely big, slow, and subject to mass failure.

Inconsistent business processes also impact labour reporting. Distinct locations or organizational divisions can have separate policies and procedures. Variances can also occur between internal labour types, such as union versus non-union, or overtime-eligible versus -ineligible. Differences can be as simple as rate or maximum work hours per day, but can also include distinct . . .

- processing and reporting deadlines,
- timesheet systems,
- accounting systems, and
- project structure requirements.

Another complicating factor is the relationship between the resource and the organization. There are separate calculations and business processes used when recording employee labour versus contracted staff augmentation efforts. Real-life examples include . . .

- The data structure for the resource name field was not consistent between timesheet systems. This required additional data transformation to prepare consolidated reports.
- Contractors and employees did not have the same week ending date for timesheet submissions. This resulted in a timing variance that needed to be managed.
- Overhead allocations for employees and contractors were not reported in the same manner. Amounts related to contract labour were identified at a resource level, while employee charges were calculated based on the total labour expenses within a specific task.

- Contractor costs were recorded to the general ledger in two accounts—the amount paid to the contractor and the fee paid to the agency. Here, the two numbers had to be added together to calculate total charges by resource and period.
- Contract resource names and time periods worked were recorded as the accounting entry description. The information needed to be extracted before being matched to project records.

As supporting systems have differing data structures and requirements, it is common to see variances as outlined above. The consolidation of these records requires an extract, transform, and load (ETL) process to align the data for use in project reporting.

C. FTE VERSUS HEADCOUNT

Full-time equivalent (FTE) is a popular labour resource measure. The FTE equates the total hours to the equal number of full-time employees required to perform the work. This calculation should be performed on a location-by-location basis to ensure that the result is not impacted by regional variances. The FTE calculation is the sum of the total hours for each location divided by the full-time hours for a single employee in the same location. The regional FTE results are then added together to calculate the measure.

I have been in projects where the leadership used full-time equivalent interchangeably with the headcount measurement. These are absolutely not the same thing. Headcount is the actual count of positions in a project each period. There is a one-to-one relationship between the headcount positions and the project staffing plan that should be provided to HR. A headcount is a simple count of active positions, there is no change in methodology based on location. FTE calculations are normally lower than headcount statistics.

75% Effort   100% Effort   50% Effort   90% Effort

Headcount = 4 Resources
Full-time Equivalent = 0.75 + 1.00 + 0.50 + 0.90 = 3.15

Figure 6-3: FTE versus headcount

To reduce confusion, I recommend including both metrics in labour resource reporting. This approach removes the potential for miscommunications and provides additional insights for stakeholders.

The difference between these metrics should be discussed and fully understood by project leadership during the planning phase. The use of FTE numbers to support detailed position planning conversations can result in the approval of reduced staffing levels. This error can be an absolute nightmare to resolve later in the project.

These calculations are also undertaken as part of the monthly reporting cycle. Staffing changes are a routine occurrence and differences between the budget and forecast are expected. However, variances in the summary metric are supported by change documentation. The explanations normally include staff turnover, the addition of resources, hiring delays, and project extensions.

D. MAXIMUM RESOURCE HOURS

It is common in labour-intensive projects to receive a plan that includes an estimate of weekly hours per resource. These assessments can be produced by either internal or external parties and are used to support project planning activities and contract negotiations.

There are a couple of inherent issues with this type of resource plan:

- Many are maintained manually within spreadsheets. For long-term, labour-intensive resource projects these weekly schedules require significant efforts to update and maintain. Further, these documents are susceptible to data entry errors.
- In some cases, a single line item may contain hours for more than one resource but is counted as one position. Often this is obvious, as the weekly hours are a factor of the maximum. This presentation will not impact FTE calculations, but headcount statistics may be inaccurate.
- There are a considerable number of variances, as common leave types are excluded in these presentations. Traditionally, maximum working hours per week are equal to paid hours per week.

On the surface, it seems reasonable the total paid hours should be the basis for estimating the project hours and cost. However, general holiday, vacation, and other leave types are normally considered in billing or overhead rates. As a result, including all paid hours and then applying the project or billing rate results in a double accounting for leaves and, therefore, an overstatement of labour estimates.

When I have had this discussion, the argument made to contradict my logic is that the standard practice allows for overtime. OK, I can see that, but I am never comfortable with this position. First, from an ethical and planning perspective, why would these additional efforts be buried in the schedule? Isn't it better to identify overtime requirements? If the project team approached planning that way, positions subject to excessive efforts could be reconfigured. This would reduce stress on resources and potential delivery bottlenecks. Second, all project estimates, particularly fixed-price bids, carry a contingency factor that could cover overtime requirements.

In my career, I have used a different approach and will refer to this as the average effort or hours method. This calculation restates the maximum daily efforts as an average of the total available working hours in the year.

Figure 6-4 provides a calculation of this maximum hours variance based on a company that observes twelve general holidays in the year, provides its employees with a benefit of one paid day off per month, and with a project team that has an average vacation entitlement of three weeks per year. In this example, the difference between the standard annual paid hours (2,088) and the actual hours eligible for project efforts (1,776) is almost eight weeks.

Days in Year	365	Total Project Hours/Resource	1,776
Less Saturday & Sunday	(104)	Weeks/Year	52
Paid Days	**261**	Average Project Hours/Week	34.15
Less General Holidays	(12)	**Average Project Hours/Day**	**6.83**
Less Corporate Days Off	(12)		
Average Vacation Days	(15)		
Project Working Days	**222**		
Hours/Day	8		
Total Project Hours/Resource	**1,776**		

Figure 6-4: Calculation for average project labour hours per day

Other non-project eligible time, including training activities or sick days, can further reduce the number of working hours available each year. This value can also be influenced by seasonal impacts or planned work stoppages. An average overtime expectation could be reflected in the calculation. This would adjust the estimate to include overtime expectations and enable related variance reporting.

This average method to determine maximum daily hours allows for a closer approximation of real labour usage. Annual variances are managed within an efficiency line item, but the hours and costs tend to be closer to the actual at year end.

Ignoring overtime factors, the difference in the approach could indicate a future schedule variance of eight weeks per project year. At an average rate of $100 per hour, the standard approach would result in an annual cost that is higher by $31,200 per full-time resource. Assuming a time-and-materials basis, the schedule delay would not immediately trigger any concerns, just a shifting of labour costs. However, schedule delays can impact other project expenses, including interest, so understanding the effect is important to forecasting efforts.

Maybe you are thinking, *so what?* Labour is managed and paid hourly; this is not important. Now, imagine that the traditional approach is used to support negotiations for a fixed-rate contract. The terms of this contract include an average hourly rate of $300 per hour, a 2 percent annual inflationary increase, and a 10 percent contingency for a five-year fixed-rate bid. In this scenario, the total implied cost overage for the 312 hours is $535,808 per resource, as the calculation in Figure 6-5 demonstrates. If there were twenty resources on this project, this variance would equate to more than $10 million.

	Year 1	Year 2	Year 3	Year 4	Year 5	Total
Hours Variance	312	312	312	312	312	**1,560**
Hourly Rate (2% Annual Increase)	$ 300	$ 306	$ 312	$ 318	$ 325	
Annual Cost	$ 93,600	$ 95,472	$ 97,381	$ 99,329	$ 101,316	**$ 487,098**
10% Contingency	$ 9,360	$ 9,547	$ 9,738	$ 9,933	$ 10,132	**$ 48,710**
Total Cost	**$ 102,960**	**$ 105,019**	**$ 107,120**	**$ 109,262**	**$ 111,447**	**$ 535,808**

Figure 6-5: Annual hour variance cost impact calculation

Note that I use the phrasing "implied cost overage." Clarification is required to understand why the additional 312 annual hours are included. This could be an actual cost estimation overage. Alternately, these hours could be related to a potential schedule variance or the inclusion of undefined overtime allowances. Further, for short-term projects, there may be no variance, as the team is expected to work for the duration of the project, with leave being provided after completion.

The additional hours under a standard approach may also include allowances for staff turnover activities. Deeper conversations on this topic could lead to confrontation between an organization and a third-party supplier. Typically, the vendor will want to account for all costs related to the project, including the transition activities. Should these additional expenses be shared between the parties? Is the transition cost directly attributable to project efforts or is it a normal-course business activity? These considerations should be included in initial contract discussions.

As you can see, understanding how maximum labour hours are calculated can have a significant impact on costing efforts. However, the project schedule and deliverables must be considered in this analysis. The answer could be related to clarification of the underlying assumptions.

E. ADDITIONAL LABOUR CONSIDERATIONS

1. Project Labour Rates

Project labour rates will be dependent on the nature of the initiative. However, these rates normally include a base pay and an overhead or burden component. The base would represent the actual cost of the labour, including the total salary and the benefits for the position. For clarity, the general holiday and vacation pay entitlements are included in this amount. The burden component represents the cost of the overhead and operating expenses attributable to the role. Finally, the total cost is divided by the expected number of billable hours per year. Internal project rates reflect a fully burdened amount, and there is not an added profit component.

$$\text{Project Rate} = \frac{\text{Salary} + \text{Benefits}}{\text{Billable Hours}} = \frac{\$75,000 \text{ Salary} + 20\% \text{ Benefits}}{1,776 \text{ Hours}}$$

$$= \frac{\$75,000 \times 120\%}{1,776} = \frac{\$90,000}{1,776}$$

$$= \$50.68/\text{Hour}$$

Figure 6-6: Project rate calculation

It must be mentioned that there are circumstances where the burden factors must be reviewed and adjusted based on project type. For example, internally developed software projects require the removal of specific overhead costs from the calculation. In these situations, it may even be possible for a single role to have two rates on the same project, dependent on the nature of their work. For example, the role could have a reduced rate for application development but be charged at full cost for related hardware implementation activities.

If the project is a service agreement, a profit target or multiplier will be added to the fully burdened rate. This amount will reflect the desired profit margin for the organization. As a reminder, the profit goal will always be reflected as 100 percent of the calculated rate, plus the desired return. In the case of external contracts, this rate will be charged to all client initiatives and adjustments are not required.

$$
\begin{aligned}
\text{Bill Rate} \ &= \ \text{Project Rate x Profit Goal} \\
&= \ \$50.68/\text{Hours x 125\% Profit Goal} \\
&= \ \$63.35/\text{Hours}
\end{aligned}
$$

Figure 6-7: Billing rate calculation

2. Hidden Operating Costs

When reviewing proposals for a labour-based capital project, the plan may contain undisclosed operating activities. The project controller will need to identify these costs and ensure the reporting structure will accommodate both the capital and operating efforts. This would include budget, forecast, and actual reporting processes. It also includes timesheet and project general ledger set up.

These operating costs are not always easy to identify. It requires understanding the nature of the project and the underlying processes associated with the delivery. Even then, further clarity on the tasks may be needed.

The best example of this concept is a software development project. In these endeavours, charges relating to data conversion, user training, and certain overheads are not eligible for capitalization. When preparing the budget or working through contract negotiations, it is common to see staffing plans with a list of roles and associated hourly efforts aligned to a delivery schedule. Although there may be summaries for the planned hours and costs, the operational activities are normally not separated from capital efforts. The project controller needs to work with internal and external teams to ensure the operating tasks are clearly defined as part of the planning process.

To complicate this, an undertaking that would seem to be an operating component may still have a capital impact. For example, efforts expended to develop a data extraction and conversion tool could be considered capital, as the tool becomes an asset to the company. However, the costs to perform the data conversion activities is purely operational.

It is the responsibility of both the project controller and manager to recognize these types of issues. They should then consult with the company's internal experts to ensure costs are correctly allocated between the balance sheet and income statement. These intricate breakdowns between capital and operating components are often missed during the planning phase.

Early identification of these allocations, paired with continuous monitoring throughout delivery, will reduce overhead and audit costs associated with reviewing and reassigning the costs at the end of the project.

F. PROJECT IMPACTS OF LABOUR COSTING DECISIONS

Anyone that has supported a labour-intensive project knows the reporting can be extremely complex and that there are different approaches to capturing the costs. Surprisingly, different methods can be used simultaneously within the same organization. When I have encountered these inconsistencies, the approach was at the project manager's discretion, as methodology was not covered within company policy.

This is an area that can be used to manipulate performance metrics. Throughout my career, I have regularly seen project managers and owners intimidate staff into working unreported overtime hours. These undisclosed and unpaid hours were used to keep the project on schedule and on budget. Many resources were worked passed the point of exhaustion.

This discussion focuses on how labour efforts and costs can be reported. For hourly and overtime eligible resources, it will be assumed that the hours worked are equal to the submitted hours. However, treatment of costs for overtime-exempt, salaried employees will be explored. These resources are compensated for a base number of hours. If overtime is reported, actual efforts to complete the project can be tracked. As they are not paid for additional work hours, the cost of the project could be overstated dependent on the allocation process.

The method chosen should be standardized by the organization, not left to the discretion of individual project managers. This will normalize corporate reporting and reduce the opportunity for the manipulation of project results. However, internal project costs may not provide sufficient benchmarking information. The organization should consider these requirements, as benchmarking influences the planning for future solutions.

The more popular labour recognition methods are summarized in the following tables. To reiterate, these examples are limited to reporting for overtime-exempt, salaried employees.

Actual Hours, Standard Project Rate			
Complexity	**Privacy**	**Effort Matching**	**Cost Matching**
😐	🙂	🙂	🙁
Medium	Good	Good	Poor
Description	• All hours worked are reported. • Costs are assigned at pre-determined project rates.		
Pros	• Matches hours to project deliverables. • Identifies over- or under-use of labour resources. • Reduces complexity in rate tracking. • Salary information is confidential.		
Cons	• Pre-determined rates result in a variance from actual corporate cost. • Can create the appearance of profits or losses from labour allocations.		

Standard Project Hours, Standard Project Rate			
Complexity	**Privacy**	**Effort Matching**	**Cost Matching**
🙂	🙂	🙁	🙁
Low	Good	Poor	Poor
Description	• Hours are reported as pre-determined maximum hours per day. • Costs are assigned at pre-determined project rate.		
Pros	• Reduces variance to the actual resource cost. • Reduces complexity for hours reporting, forecasting, and rate tracking. • Salary information is confidential.		
Cons	• No visibility to actual efforts and cost used to complete project deliverables. • Can lead to overuse and burnout of resources.		

Actual Hours, Actual Labour Rate			
Complexity	Privacy	Effort Matching	Cost Matching
☹	☹	☺	☺
High	Poor	Good	Good

Description	• All worked hours are reported. • Actual costs are assigned at individual resource rates.
Pros	• Matches hours and costs to project deliverables. • Identifies over- or under-use of labour resources.
Cons	• Salary information is not confidential. • Complex to track and report.

Standard Project Hours, Actual Labour Rate			
Complexity	Privacy	Effort Matching	Cost Matching
😐	☹	☹	😐
Medium	Poor	Poor	Medium

Description	• Hours are reported as pre-determined maximum hours per day. • Actual costs are assigned at individual resource rates.
Pros	• Reduces the variance to the actual cost of a resource. • Reduces the complexity for hours reporting and forecasting.
Cons	• No visibility to actual efforts used to complete project deliverables. • Can lead to overuse and burnout of resources. • Salary information is not confidential. • Tracking and reporting salary information remains complex.

Actual Hours, Standard Project Rate Periodic Adjustment to Actual Labour Cost			
Complexity	**Privacy**	**Effort Matching**	**Cost Matching**
😐	😐	🙂	🙂
Medium	**Medium**	**Good**	**Good**
Description	• All worked hours are reported. • Costs are assigned at pre-determined project rates. • Periodic adjustments are made to restate allocated labour cost to actual cost.		
Pros	• Matches hours and costs to project deliverables. • Identifies over- or under-use of labour resources. • Reduces complexity in rate tracking.		
Cons	• Partial sharing of salary data for the purposes of calculating adjustments. • Periodic valuation issues. • Additional efforts required to calculate adjustment from allocated to actual costs.		

Factors such as alternative pay arrangements, corporate overhead allocations, location of work, internal versus external resourcing, schedule changes, and foreign exchange add to the complexity of labour reporting and benchmarking activities.

Organizations need to consider the above when establishing their project framework. Is it important to understand the real execution costs? Perhaps this consideration is secondary to minimizing project reporting efforts. If determining the value of execution is subordinate to other corporate objectives, is there a process for recognizing the variance when planning future endeavours? Without a follow-up mechanism, subsequent project evaluations will be flawed.

G. THE INFLUENCE OF LABOUR COST COMPONENTS

The labour reporting choices discussed in the prior section can also affect other aspects of corporate reporting.

For example, the decision to report employee costs on actual project hours using standard rates could result in excessive internal charges. This would be reflected as a negative overhead cost in the associated operating department. In effect, the operational view would appear as additional profits within the organization. If this impact is not considered, the net income of the company could be overstated.

Many unit charges are based on blended rates – they include multiple costing components. Equipment rates include labour, overhead allocations, and direct operational expenses. Estimates for material installation, such as underground utilities, are provided based on expected quantities. These unit rates would include the same component costs as equipment. Blended rates are also affected by the labour choices, which could impact consumer pricing in addition to corporate returns. If the labour cost decision impacts a company's ability to maintain competitive pricing, customers will look to other organizations for solutions to their business needs.

When blended rates are examined, project staff should be able to discuss the overall result and variances arising from each of the individual components. Stakeholders could be looking for ways to reduce external pricing and maintain market positioning. In this situation, reliance on high-level analyses may not be sufficient to enable strategic decisions.

7. LABOUR – BUDGETS, FORECASTS, AND ACTUAL REPORTING

The concepts discussed in the next two chapters are related to internal labour efforts, including contracted staff augmentation resources. The activities of this workforce are directly controlled by the company that owns the project.

Third-party contract reporting is covered in Chapter 9. These are arrangements where an external vendor directs the day-to-day tasks of the resource team. However, many of the internal labour concepts can be adapted to manage supplier contracts that are billed on an hourly basis.

A. LABOUR ASSUMPTIONS

1. BUDGET ASSUMPTIONS

It is necessary to maintain clear documentation of the assumptions used in labour calculations. From the initial project discussions to the preparation of the functional budget, these statements will change dramatically. Each new budget revision should add detail and clarify prior estimates. These will be the basis for preparing labour summaries, variance explanations, and KPI reports.

After the project is initiated, labour metrics and HR processes will be tied to each budgeted position. The actual project positions will be configured to match the resource level, efforts, and service location as outlined in the assumptions. Identifying individual roles as part of planning reduces confusion and reporting efforts during the delivery phase.

Standard categories that should be defined in the budget are as follows:

- The budget role, including a unique identifier (ID) and a descriptive title. The ID will be used to match the role to future forecast and actual results.
- The start and end dates, which identify when the resource is expected to be on the project.
- The average effort, in percent, the role is expected to use on the project. This is applied to the daily maximum hours to calculate budget hours.
- The organizational relationship, which defines the employment arrangement between the resource and the company (employee, contractor, intern, etc.).
- The geographic delivery location for the proposed role, which can impact calculations for base hours and rates.

In addition to these, the budget rate must be included in the assumptions. This can be accomplished in several ways:

- If the rate is tied to a specific pay level, a level category should be added for each role. This field would then be matched to a standard rate for each unique category.
- If the rate has both a base and an overhead component, these can be identified individually or combined to create a single rate.

- Expected rate changes should be included in the assumptions, either using additional fields or calculated using an applied inflation/deflation rate.
- If a foreign location is involved, any exchange factor used in converting the foreign rate to the reporting currency must be documented. This assumption could be different for capital and operating activities.

PM1 – Project Manager	DM1 – Delivery Manager
Jan. 5, 20xx to Apr. 20, 20xx: 75% Effort	Feb. 15, 20xx to Aug. 1, 20xx: 15% Effort
Apr. 21, 20xx to Sep. 25, 20xy: 100% Effort	Aug. 2, 20xx to Apr. 17, 20xy: 75% Effort
Employee – Toronto Office	Apr. 18, 20xy to Aug. 15, 20xy: 50% Effort
Senior Manager – Rate $250/Hr	Contractor – Houston Office
	Manager – Rate $175/Hr
	Foreign Exchange = 1.3000

Figure 7-1: Budget labour assumptions

Assumptions must be secured for each budget or subsequent revision. Once a budget has been approved and published, any changes must be documented and included in the forecast.

2. MULTIPLE RECORDS PER ROLE

In both the budget and forecast, a single role could require multiple records to document the assumptions. Examples of times where multiple records would exist include . . .

- If a resource is going to be used on the project, but that term will not be continuous.
- If the resource will have varied effort levels during different periods on the project. This assumption could be documented as individual records or as an average effort for the duration.

- If the resource is expected to relocate during the project delivery schedule.
- If the resource is expected to have a rate change that is not in line with standard project assumptions. This could include promotions or contract renewals.
- If multiple individuals will fill the role.

Each record forms part of the overall assumptions relating to the position, and changes become part of the variance explanation.

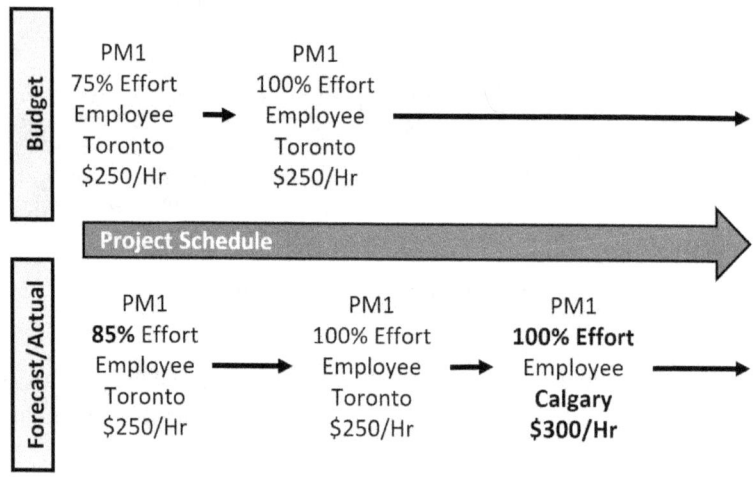

Figure 7-2: Labour resource assumption changes

Labour buckets are special considerations and will be discussed in a later section.

3. FORECAST AND ACTUAL ASSUMPTIONS

Both the forecast and actual results are based on the latest project updates. As such, a single record of these current assumptions will apply to both. For simplicity, this section will refer to these as *forecast* assumptions.

Standard categories that should be defined for each role in the fore-cast are as follows:

- The forecast role, including a unique ID and descriptive title.
- If the role is in the original budget, the Budget ID. If the position did not exist in the budget, this field would be blank or flagged as a new position.
- The resource name and if available, ID, which will be included to tie the forecast information into timesheet reporting and incurred costs.
- The position number and status, which is used to coordinate with human resources. Typical status indicators include filled, vacant, recruiting, and off-board. A position may be marked as cancelled if budgeted and no longer required. "Transferred" can be used if a budgeted position is moved between report-ing teams.
- The start and end dates, effort, organization relationship, and location fields also exist in the forecast assumptions. These have the same purpose and definition as they do in the budget, but the underlying assumptions may be different.
- The rate information must also be maintained. These assump-tions should be documented in the same manner as they were for the budget.

Contractor positions are normally estimated at one rate or based on specific levels. During the delivery phase, there are different rates and effective dates for each contractor that need to be managed. The value of the corresponding rate variance can significantly impact project expenses.

PM1 – Project Manager	DM1 – Delivery Manager
Budget ID = PM1	Budget ID = DM1
Arianna Stone	**Name TBD**
Jan. 5, 20xx to **Jun. 15**, 20xx: **85%** Effort	Feb. 15, 20xx to Aug. 1, 20xx: 15% Effort
Jun. 16, 20xx to **Sep. 10, 20xx:** 100% Effort	Aug. 2, 20xx to Apr. 17, 20xy: 75% Effort
Employee – **Offboard** – Toronto Office	Apr. 18, 20xy to Aug. 15, 20xy: 50% Effort
Senior Manager – Rate $250/Hr	Contractor – **Recruiting** – Houston Office
Joe Smith	**Market** – Rate **$157**/Hr
Sep. 20xx to Sep. 25, 20xy: 00% Effort	Foreign Exchange = **1.3200**
Employee – **Filled** – **Calgary Office**	
Partner Level – Rate **$300/Hr**	

Figure 7-3: Forecast and budget assumption variances

For the purposes of forecast and actual reporting, the foreign exchange rate moves to a periodic rather than overarching project assumption. Incurred periods are recorded at the historic rates, while forecast periods use the latest corporate assumptions for foreign exchange. Note that the forecast and budget rates may not be equivalent.

	Actual Month 7	Actual Month 8	Actual Month 9	Forecast Month 10	Forecast Month 11	Forecast Month 12
FX Rate - Budget	1.3000	1.3000	1.3000	1.3000	1.3000	1.3000
FX Rate - Forecast	**1.2818**	**1.3139**	**1.3861**	**1.3200**	**1.3200**	**1.3200**

Figure 7-4: Periodic foreign exchange run rates

Review of the forecast assumptions should happen on a recurring basis—preferably monthly prior to accrual submission. The corresponding modifications should be reflected in the appropriate documentation as outlined in the "Labour Change Orders" section.

4. MANAGING LABOUR BUCKETS

Sometimes, line-item placeholders are created for efforts that are expected from multiple part-time resources. An example would be an allowance for quarterly meetings of Subject Matter Experts (SMEs).

These labour "buckets" can skew resource reporting efforts.

- If not identified as a member of the bucket, these resources are normally shown as unplanned overages.
- If included in the budget headcount calculation, the line would count as a single person, when multiple resources are expected.
- As actuals are incurred, including the multiple resources in the headcount calculation can create peaks in resourcing statistics.
- Although not as dramatic as headcount impact, calculations for project FTEs are also inflated by these part-time efforts.

Preferably, these resources are identified in advance of efforts and tied to the labour bucket line item. If the resources are first identified as unplanned efforts, re-work is required to update timesheet reports, forecast records, and variance calculations.

For clarity, it is best to exclude labour buckets from project resource calculations for FTEs and headcounts. This information could be provided as a secondary summary that focuses only on intermittent, part-time efforts.

B. LABOUR CHANGE ORDERS

This section will discuss when the formal recognition of labour modifications is required in a change order.

From a practical standpoint, labour forecasts frequently change monthly during the review and update meeting. In theory, these adjustments could require the creation of a change order each month; however, this practice may significantly increase project overhead. Organizations may choose to track these changes and prepare formal documents at specific intervals, such as quarterly instead of monthly. In addition, it is more efficient to compile related information instead of issuing a document for each change. For smaller projects, the labour change order could cover all staffing modifications in the specified period. For larger projects, change orders may be issued by team to add clarity and make tracking easier.

When there is a notable change in labour assumptions and costs, a change order should be issued as soon as possible, documenting and formalizing the change. Recognition of significant changes should not be delayed.

The following types of labour adjustments should be included:

- changes to start or end dates,
- changes to efforts or total hours,
- changes to levels or rates,
- changes to the location of a resource,
- the addition of resources,
- the cancellation of positions,
- positions that are transferred between teams within the project, and
- permanent run rate variances.

If the organization is using the average effort method and all other assumptions remain equal to the budget, variances arising from the difference between the actual and average hours are not permanent until either the end of the year or the project—whichever is shorter.

The overall project environment must also be considered when calculating costs. If the project is subject to interest, every labour change order must include an associated interest impact. Figure 7-5 shows that although the labour cost does not change at the first review, there is a $200 cost savings as total project interest is reduced. This change may also indicate that there has been a delay to the overall project schedule.

	M6	M7	M8	M9	M10	M11	M12	M1	Total
Budget									
Hours	160	160	160	160	160	160	-	-	960
Rate/Hour	$ 50	$ 50	$ 50	$ 50	$ 50	$ 50	$ 50	$ 55	
Labour Cost	$ 8,000	$ 8,000	$ 8,000	$ 8,000	$ 8,000	$ 8,000	$ -	$ -	$ 48,000
Interest @ 5%	$ 33	$ 67	$ 100	$ 133	$ 167	$ 200	$ 200	$ 200	$ 1,100
Total Cost	$ 8,033	$ 8,067	$ 8,100	$ 8,133	$ 8,167	$ 8,200	$ 200	$ 200	$ 49,100
Review 1 - Resource Start Delayed by 1 Month									
Hours	-	160	160	160	160	160	160	-	960
Rate/Hour	$ 50	$ 50	$ 50	$ 50	$ 50	$ 50	$ 50	$ 55	
Labour Cost	$ -	$ 8,000	$ 8,000	$ 8,000	$ 8,000	$ 8,000	$ 8,000	$ -	$ 48,000
Interest @ 5%	$ -	$ 33	$ 67	$ 100	$ 133	$ 167	$ 200	$ 200	$ 900
Total Cost	$ -	$ 8,033	$ 8,067	$ 8,100	$ 8,133	$ 8,167	$ 8,200	$ 200	$ 48,900
						Net Savings From Change ($49,100 - $48,900)		$	200
Review 2 - Resource Extended by 1 Month									
Hours	-	160	160	160	160	160	160	160	1,120
Rate/Hour	$ 50	$ 50	$ 50	$ 50	$ 50	$ 50	$ 50	$ 55	
Labour Cost	$ -	$ 8,000	$ 8,000	$ 8,000	$ 8,000	$ 8,000	$ 8,000	$ 8,800	$ 56,800
Interest @ 5%	$ -	$ 33	$ 67	$ 100	$ 133	$ 167	$ 200	$ 237	$ 937
Total Cost	$ -	$ 8,033	$ 8,067	$ 8,100	$ 8,133	$ 8,167	$ 8,200	$ 9,037	$ 57,737
						Net Increase From Change ($48,900 - $57,737)		$	(8,837)

Figure 7-5: Impact of schedule changes to cost estimates

At the second review point, the resource is extended adding $8,800 in labour costs and $37 in interest charges. This change also impacts year-over-year budget allocations and could be a further indication of a delayed project.

As this simple example demonstrates, it is important the controller has a thorough understanding of the entire project environment. Changes to the forecast impact a variety of components, including scheduling and carrying costs.

C. ACTUAL, FORECAST, AND BUDGET LAYOUTS

The layout for the budget, forecast, and actual reporting should remain consistent. Typically, these contain sections for both hours reporting and cost calculations. The cost may also be broken into separate sections for base rate and burden calculations. For the most accurate variance reporting, this data should contain detailed records by resource and role. The following table provides a summary of the differences between each of these project views. As discussed throughout this chapter, these costs, and the associated variances, need to be managed for each resource record.

	Budget	**Forecast**	**Actual**
Hours	Estimated	Incurred + Estimated *(Changes to prior periods)*	Accrued + Estimated *(No changes to prior periods)*
Costs	Budget Hours x Budget Rate	Forecast Hours x Forecast Rate	Accrued Hours x Forecast Rate
Accrual Value			Total Estimated - Incurred *(Both costs and hours)*

Depending on the nature and complexity of the project, the tracking may also need to be broken down into teams or individual tasks. When the complexity of the project increases, so will the number of data points and work segments that need to be managed.

What if a budget only has summary information? How is this addressed in a variance calculation? The inclusion of a schedule view can assist in determining if the variance is attributable to hours or schedule changes. In the calculation outlined in Figure 7-6, the hours variance is an overage of $14,000, the schedule variance is $12,400. The project rate variance cannot be calculated as the budget did not include individual rate assumptions.

	M8	M9	M10	M11	M12	Total
Class 5						
Schedule						
Total Cost	$ 25,000	$ 25,000	$ 25,000	$ 25,000	$ -	$ 100,000
Class 2						
Schedule						
Hours						
Resource 1	160	160	160	160	-	640
Resource 2	160	160	160	160	160	800
Resource 3	80	80	80	80	80	400
Resource 4	160	160	160	160	-	640
Total Hours	560	560	560	560	240	3,440
Cost						
Resource 1 @ $50/Hr	$ 8,000	$ 8,000	$ 8,000	$ 8,000	$ -	$ 32,000
Resource 2 @ $40/Hr	$ 6,400	$ 6,400	$ 6,400	$ 6,400	$ 6,400	$ 32,000
Resource 3 @ $75/Hr	$ 6,000	$ 6,000	$ 6,000	$ 6,000	$ 6,000	$ 30,000
Resource 4 @ $50/Hr	$ 8,000	$ 8,000	$ 8,000	$ 8,000	$ -	$ 32,000
Total Cost	$ 28,400	$ 28,400	$ 28,400	$ 28,400	$ 12,400	$ 126,000

Cost Variance
($28,400 – $25,000) x 4 = $13,600

Schedule Variance

Figure 7-6: Labour variance from a summary budget

D. RUN RATE METRICS

These are summary metrics that provide a quick comparison between the actual, forecast, and budget information.

Best practice would be to include a project timeline for each section. This provides a visual to outline any schedule variances since the budget was prepared. The budget timeline is a static picture—it does not change. The actual and forecast section have the same timeline, which is modified based on updates to the project schedule. These graphics could be displayed in a single line, but it may be helpful to have different program phases in different lines, as activities for multiple deliverables can overlap.

The run rate metrics that should be brought forward for each period are the total cost, total hours, full-time equivalent resources, and headcount. These metrics can be provided at a project level but may be further defined by including team or location breakdowns.

	Actual	Actual	Actual	Actual
Month Ending	Jan-31	Feb-28	Mar-31	Apr-30
FX Rate - Actual & Forecast	1.2719	1.2698	1.2496	1.2792
FX Rate - Budget	1.3000	1.3000	1.3000	1.3000
FTE is rounded to 0.25 of employee				
ACTUAL/FORECAST METRICS				
Project Timeline				
Project Cost	$ 61,537.50	$ 74,064.85	$ 114,313.76	$ 82,970.49
Internal Cost	$ 22,543.60	$ 23,522.12	$ 43,173.85	$ 24,136.82
Project Hours	373.50	365.00	580.75	430.50
Internal Hours	371.75	362.00	579.25	426.75
Full Time Equivalent	2.00	2.25	2.50	2.50
Headcount (Resource Count)	9.00	10.00	10.00	11.00
FORECAST METRICS				
Project Timeline				
Project Cost	$ 58,287.26	$ 74,096.26	$ 89,374.17	$ 82,011.52
Internal Cost	$ 21,157.12	$ 24,524.50	$ 34,652.85	$ 25,225.82
Project Hours	334.00	378.00	447.00	415.00
Internal Hours	334.00	378.00	447.00	415.00
Full Time Equivalent	2.00	2.25	2.50	2.50
Headcount (Resource Count)	9.00	10.00	10.00	11.00
BUDGET METRICS				
Project Timeline				
Project Cost	$ 305,604.34	$ 290,886.75	$ 343,511.44	$ 320,965.84
Internal Cost	$ 89,604.63	$ 85,320.13	$ 99,955.43	$ 92,783.41
Project Hours	1,282.50	1,221.00	1,424.75	1,317.75
Internal Hours	1,299.00	1,237.00	1,441.75	1,332.50
Full Time Equivalent	7.50	7.50	7.50	7.75
Headcount (Resource Count)	10.00	10.00	10.00	10.00

Figure 7-7: Run rate metric report

The period for the metrics is also important to understand. For example, if monthly reporting periods are summarized on a quarterly or annual basis, the FTE and headcount calculations are most appropriately based on the average. This would create variances to the monthly data.

Run rate schedules provide project managers with a single point of reference to quickly compare labour performance. Further, these values can be used to provide estimates for proposed schedule changes. These evaluations would be subject to clarification and formalization but are handy for preliminary discussions.

E. LABOUR VARIANCES

Providing variances at a position level can assist the project management team in understanding the efficiency of resources. This practice can also identify gaps between the budget assumptions and current resource performance.

Role ID	Role Title	Actual		Forecast		Variance	
		Hours	Cost	Hours	Cost	Hours	Cost
LABOUR VARIANCE		**6,717.00**	**$ 1,423,461**	**6,635.00**	**$ 1,410,426**	**(82.00)**	**$ (13,036)**
DATA-001	Data Manager	555.50	$ 111,100	539.00	$ 107,800	(16.50)	$ (3,300)
DATA-002	Analyst 1	807.50	$ 201,875	800.00	$ 200,000	(7.50)	$ (1,875)
DATA-003	Analyst 2	731.50	$ 95,450	723.00	$ 94,468	(8.50)	$ (982)
INT-001	Integration Manager	709.75	$ 138,284	701.00	$ 136,239	(8.75)	$ (2,045)
INT-002	Analyst 1	609.00	$ 60,900	594.00	$ 59,400	(15.00)	$ (1,500)
INT-003	Analyst 2	771.25	$ 100,637	758.00	$ 98,611	(13.25)	$ (2,025)
OCM-001	Change Mgmt Manager	-	$ -	-	$ -	-	$ -
PMO-001	Project Manager	471.75	$ 141,525	481.00	$ 144,300	9.25	$ 2,775
PMO-002	Project Admin	970.00	$ 301,003	970.00	$ 302,358	-	$ 1,354
PMO-003	Project Controller	529.25	$ 132,313	515.00	$ 128,750	(14.25)	$ (3,563)
SEC-001	Security Resource	561.50	$ 140,375	554.00	$ 138,500	(7.50)	$ (1,875)
Expense Forecast			$ 71,189		$ 71,189		$ -
Contingency			$ -		$ -		$ -
Adjust To Fixed Rate Contract			$ -		$ -		$ -
TOTAL		**6,717.00**	**$ 1,494,650**	**6,635.00**	**$ 1,481,614**	**(82.00)**	**$ (13,036)**

Figure 7-8: Labour variance report

Figure 7-8 demonstrates a sample variance calculation by role for an information technology project. This report identifies each position and provides the associated hours and cost variance from the budget or forecast. Explanations for the variances should also be included as part of the discussion.

The labour cost variance can be shown as an overall value or can be further broken into components. These component costs will provide better insight into the factors that are driving financial changes to the project:

1) The rate variance is the difference between the budgeted and actual rates charged to the program. It is calculated as (Forecast Rate - Budget Rate) x Budget Hours. The rate may include a foreign exchange component. Depending on the organization, these exchange variances may need to be reported separately from base labour rates.

2) The hours variance is the difference between the budgeted hours and the actual hours charged to the program. Typically, these are normal course-of-business variances (vacation, sick leave, general holidays). The formula for the hours variance is (Forecast Hours - Budget Hours) x Budget Rate. This calculation excludes any changes to schedule duration.

3) The schedule variance captures the cost difference between the forecast and budgeted duration. These are intentional changes to the length of a resource's schedule, such as delaying the start of a resource or extending the service time on the project.

4) Other position changes that may be captured include new positions, transfers between teams (budget reallocation), and the cancelations of budgeted positions. If these changes are reported, they should be reflected as separate line items, as there are usually larger resourcing discussions involved.

Role ID	Role Title	Breakdown of Cost Variance (Budget to Forecast)					Total
		Rate Variance	Hours Variance	Schedule Variance	New Positions	Timing Variance	
LABOUR VARIANCE		$ (194,221)	$2,278,305	$ 299,880	$ (95,450)	$ (13,036)	$ 2,275,479
DATA-001	Data Manager	$ -	$ 357,500	$ -	$ -	$ (3,300)	$ 354,200
DATA-002	Analyst 1	$ (631,275)	$ 852,125	$ -	$ -	$ (1,875)	$ 218,975
DATA-003	Analyst 2	$ -	$ 982	$ -	$ (95,450)	$ (982)	$ (95,450)
INT-001	Integration Manager	$ 121,535	$ 223,551	$ -	$ -	$ (2,045)	$ 343,041
INT-002	Analyst 1	$ 74,025	$ 187,350	$ -	$ -	$ (1,500)	$ 259,875
INT-003	Analyst 2	$ (35,029)	$ 52,818	$ -	$ -	$ (2,025)	$ 15,763
OCM-001	Change Mgmt Manager	$ -	$ -	$ -	$ -	$ -	$ -
PMO-001	Project Manager	$ 50,618	$ 957	$ 4,000	$ -	$ 2,775	$ 58,350
PMO-002	Project Admin	$ 138,618	$ (94,915)	$ 295,880	$ -	$ 1,354	$ 340,937
PMO-003	Project Controller	$ 87,288	$ 307,688	$ -	$ -	$ (3,563)	$ 391,413
SEC-001	Security Resource	$ -	$ 390,250	$ -	$ -	$ (1,875)	$ 388,375
Expense Forecast							$ 113,758
Contingency							$ 388,389
Adjust To Fixed Rate Contract							$ -
TOTAL		$ (194,221)	$2,278,305	$ 299,880	$ (95,450)	$ (13,036)	$ 2,777,626

Figure 7-9: Detailed labour variance

Note that the variance calculations only consider the changes from the budget to the forecast, and that the actual is not included. The reason for this is that differences between the actual and the forecast are traditionally associated with timing. As demonstrated, this variance can also be reported.

Although these calculations are discussed for labour reporting, a similar approach can be used to determine the variance for other project costs. For those expenses, the controller would need to identify each input and then calculate the differences between the budget and forecast. Detailed analysis of blended rate components would be managed in this manner.

One additional reporting option is a view that outlines timing versus permanent variances. This report is of particular use in multi-year programs where carry-forward requirements need to be clearly defined. To complete this report, a project controller needs to understand the origin of the variance for each position:

- Vacations that are carried forward or delays to position start dates with no change to total duration are examples of timing variances. There may be annual rate impacts, but the bulk of the difference would be reported as a variance from a change in hours.
- The practice of budgeting general holidays as working days results in a permanent variance unless a resource performs activities on those days.

8. TIMESHEETS

Timesheets, *ugh*. Personally, I *despise* filling out timesheets. It is my least favourite activity. Unfortunately, I live my life in a project world, and timesheets are my reality. Even worse, my team is usually responsible for ensuring these documents are complete and correct for the entire project. I have deep empathy for those who submit their timesheets late or do not want to do so at all.

So, why do organizations require time tracking? From a broad perspective, timesheet reporting . . .

- measures productivity,
- distributes efforts to corporate initiatives,
- increases the accuracy of billing,
- confirms payroll liabilities, and
- tracks leave entitlements.

As timesheets capture past efforts, there should not be any great mystery surrounding the data or its uses. I am, however, consistently surprised that the importance of this information is understated at a project level.

The timesheet is the tool used to track and allocate labour costs to projects. Timesheet data . . .

- confirms the accuracy of hours charged to the project,
- supports accrual calculations,
- establishes the cost charged to the program,

- confirms forecast assumptions,
- enables variance reporting,
- confirms general ledger records, and
- provides auditable evidence in support of costs.

This discussion is going to focus on the importance of timesheets with respect to allocating efforts to a capital project initiative. However, it is also applicable in an operating project or job costing situation.

A. TIMESHEET REPORT CRITERIA

All labour-based projects require a standard timesheet report. Consolidated reports with consistent requirements should be a mandatory component of an organization's project reporting structure.

The source for the report should *always* be the time entry system(s). Labour resources submit hours directly to the time entry system, so this is the location of complete data. Records from subsequent systems do not guarantee completeness. Downstream systems may be missing corrections or unapproved time entries.

In addition to employees, organizations augment their staff by using temporary contract labour. The activities of these resources are directly controlled by the company that owns the project. As such, the corporation owns the hiring decision and normally requires a direct timesheet submission. The data for these types of resources may be captured in a different system than that of the employees.

To ensure completeness of the report information, timesheet data must come from all applicable systems. This includes all employee and direct contract labour sources.

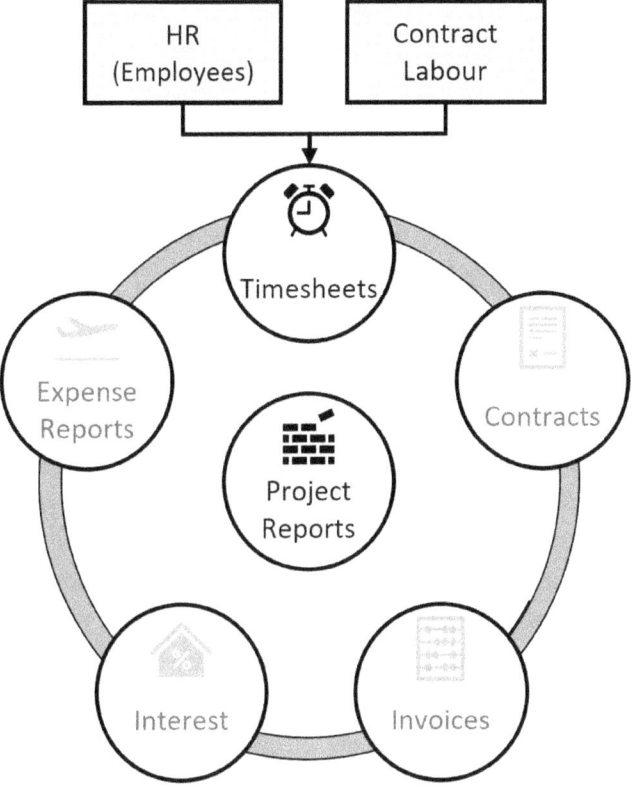

Figure 8-1: Timesheet relationship in project reporting

Timesheet data should also include all hours submitted to a project. The report should not be limited to approved time or active resources. Project labour cost is a function of the hours booked. Therefore, it is important all potential hours are identified and remain in the record. The inclusion of unapproved time entries increases the accuracy of accrual calculations and can be used in metrics for performance management.

Most organizations require weekly timesheet submission. This ensures the resource's recollection of activities is fresh. The corresponding project reports should be prepared and reviewed on a weekly basis.

One of the purposes of regular time reporting is to confirm the completeness and accuracy of the information. As such, organizations do not lock in timesheets immediately following the workweek. They allow a grace period for changing, correcting, or late data entry. As a result, the report should be generated on a project-to-date basis to ensure the completeness and accuracy of records.

Ideally, the timesheet information should be reported directly from the source system. This scenario represents the lowest opportunity for data loss or process errors.

If the data is provided in a downloaded format, file size may impact the reporting efforts. In this case, limiting time parameters to the current fiscal year can reduce files to manageable sizes. If timesheet data is broken into fiscal year reports, it is important to request a final fiscal year report after the data entry grace period ends. When the final files are received, a reconciliation between the hours reported at year end and the final timesheet report will be required. Any differences will need to be managed as part of the accrual and variance processes.

B. TIMESHEET PROCESS

Timesheet reporting is completed weekly to verify project hours—and therefore costs—as early as possible. Through regular review, errors can be identified and corrected in a timely manner. Typically, organizations incur lower costs to correct issues when they are discovered early. Further, a routine review of hours charged to a project will ensure best cost matching to periods for accounting purposes.

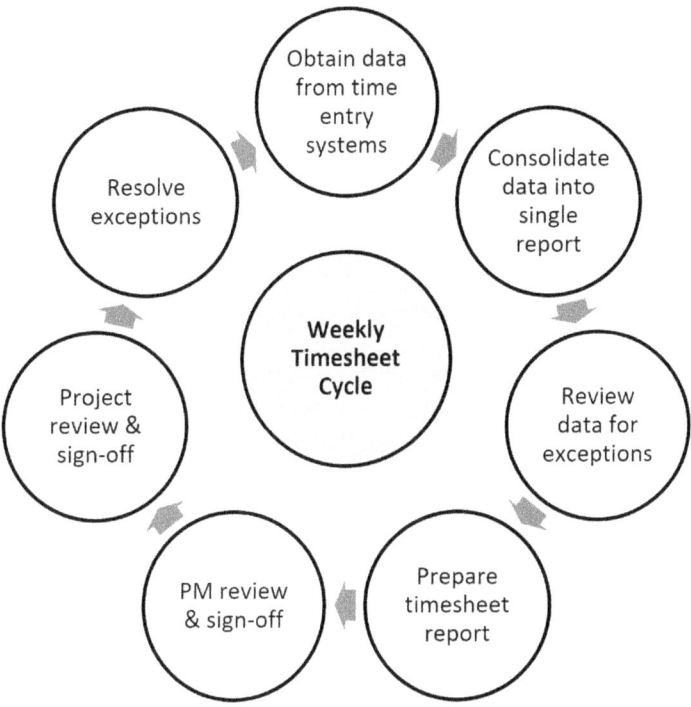

Figure 8-2: Weekly timesheet cycle

The timesheet process is simple and can be summarized in seven steps:

1) Obtain data from the time entry system(s) – Typical requirements are discussed in the "Timesheet Data Fields" section.

2) Consolidate data into a single project report – This step normally involves an ETL process to standardize and consolidate the information from all timesheet systems.

3) Review exception reporting – This is a high-level review for gross errors and is completed by the project controller.

4) Prepare the timesheet report – Consolidate timesheets in the organization's standard report format. Note any exceptions and resolution actions undertaken.

5) Obtain the project manager's review and sign-off – In this step, the project manager reviews the time report and identifies areas of concern. The project manager's sign-off is provided to confirm that the review has occurred.

6) Obtain a program review and sign-off – This step is applicable if the project is part of a larger program portfolio. This sign-off indicates management at a program level is aware of efforts to date and has been notified of any concerns.

7) Resolve exceptions – Make every effort to resolve exceptions on a weekly basis to ensure the data is corrected for the next reporting cycle.

The following sections will provide further information on timesheet process items.

C. TIMESHEET DATA FIELDS

The list below outlines the important fields in a timesheet report and describes how the information is used in project cost reporting:

1) The Resource ID is a unique identifier. From a data perspective, this number is consistent across systems and provides the best matching of records between platforms. However, this information can be considered confidential and may not be shareable with the project team.

2) The resource name is a necessity. If a Resource ID cannot be the basis to form the data relationship between systems, this connection will be based on names. Further, project managers will not recognize an ID number, they will recognize a name. Identifying labour resources by name enables the approval process.

3) The relationship between the organization and the resource is important to understand. Allowable hours or cost allocations may be different depending on terms of employment. Relationships may also impact maximum hours and rates.

4) The timesheet data report must contain either location or company fields. Labour laws may vary depending on the site the resource is working from. These differences can influence working hours, vacation entitlements, and overtime. From a cost perspective, foreign exchange may apply to calculations if the site is outside of the country.

    Business units within a single organization can also have varied labour policies. It is imperative these are identified, as this information could impact hours and cost calculations.

5) The resource position or level should be available from the system data. Many companies standardize rates based on levels, and including this field assists in confirmations.

6) Time dimensions are essential to the report. Many systems provide hours based on each date worked. Other useful periods for timesheet reporting include weekly, monthly, and yearly.

7) The Project ID and name identify the initiative within the accounting and time entry systems. It is important to capture all applicable Project IDs when requesting timesheet data. On large projects or in multinational organizations, it is common for systems to identify the same project using different numbers on local platforms.

8) Task IDs are unique within a single Project ID. These relate the efforts to the asset or work completed by a resource. As mentioned previously, tasks may be used to break projects into smaller reporting divisions.

9) The hours worked are entered by the resource. This column should include both positive and negative numbers. Negative entries indicate time entry corrections.

10) The time code field will match the reported hours to specific labour efforts. This is used to identify hours for overtime, vacations, and other potential allocation concerns.

11) Submission and approval details are also required. The project management team uses this information to follow up on outstanding timesheets. Data is the most accurate when it is submitted on time and inquiries can be resolved immediately. In addition, on-time submission and approvals increase accuracy, improve accrual estimates, and ensure costs are recognized in the appropriate accounting period.

D. DATA ETL CONSIDERATIONS

Normal data cleansing activities apply when consolidating timesheet system information into a single report. These activities include excluding null values, reviewing data types, standardizing formats, and aligning system date fields.

In addition to typical data cleansing activities, there are specific ETL considerations that apply when combining raw data from the human resource and contract labour systems:

1) The standardization of resource names is a key step. It is not unusual to see different naming conventions across multiple systems. During the ETL process, a universal name format should be applied to all data ("Last Name, First Name" or "First Name Last Name"). This transformation will create efficiency in the validation process.

Figure 8-3: Name references across systems

There can be confusion if common names are used day-to-day, as human resources and accounting database fields tend to use legal names. However, this can be managed via mapping processes.

Additional details managed through data transformation can include name changes resulting from marriage/divorce, or multiple resources with the same name.

Ideally, a Resource ID would be used in the data model to connect and confirm relationships between entry systems, costing systems, and project reports. Confidentiality could be maintained by excluding this field in the final reporting artifacts.

2)   The project Forecast and Budget IDs are add-ons to the data provided from the timesheet entry systems. The information comes directly from the project model and is attached to resource records as part of the ETL process.

This field is used to match the resource to a specific forecast or budget line item. It allows the actual hours worked to be mapped to estimates, enabling the variance reporting process.

This information may also indicate that additional tracking will be required. As discussed in the prior chapter, the need for time entry data to be broken into multiple records per resource can arise in the following situations:

   – a change in relationship with the organization,

- movement between locations or companies,
- changes in forecasted project efforts,
- rate changes, and
- enabling matching to budget or forecast records.

3) It is important to ensure applicable time periods are included as part of the data consolidation process, including standardizing date formats between systems.

Timesheet data is typically provided daily. Additional dimensions can be added during ETL to allocate the details to weeks, months, and fiscal years. This transformation allows variance analysis over distinct time dimensions.

When multiple records are required, ETL can be used to match actual hours worked to the correct Forecast ID or line item.

4) Team information, if applicable, is a subset of labour used to identify specific activities or initiatives. Typically, each team has a dedicated project or delivery manager responsible for the approval of efforts.

This is also an ETL process add-on to the raw data and comes directly from the project model. It is used to parse larger reports into streamlined approval packages. These sub-reports are then rolled up into an overall project view.

5) The Project ID and name will be included in the raw timesheet data. However, the name and number formats may need to be standardized during ETL.

If a project has multiple IDs across systems, the data consolidation should be undertaken as part of the transformation process. The original ID's can be maintained and used to enable drill-down variance reporting.

6) Like the project information, the Task ID and name will form part of the raw data set and may require standardization. These breakdowns can be used in conjunction with Project IDs to add further definition to the reports.

Details such as the resource's relationship to the organization or position/level should be extracted as part of the time entry system reports. If not, this information must be incorporated from the project model during the ETL process.

Once all extract and transform activities have been completed, the data from all source systems should be consolidated into a single project hours report. Note that additional steps may apply if the timesheet information is provided as a manual extract report, as all fields may be downloaded from the source system as text values.

E. STANDARD EXCEPTIONS

Timesheet exception reporting triggers immediate reviews and corrections to allocations. As previously discussed, early detection and action reduces overhead efforts and costs to fix errors.

The first exception review can be completed by the project controller, but the managers should also be aware of and reviewing for unusual activity.

Typical exceptions and the related standard follow-up actions are discussed below.

1) The resource cannot be tied to the project model. Generally, the individual has not been formally assigned to a role or the effort is not budgeted. These resources may belong to an allowance of hours to be used by multiple individuals.

If the efforts are valid, the project manager must link the resource to a forecast or budgeted role, a new role, or a project allowance. If the hours are invalid, the hours must be removed from the project.

2) Overtime normally requires pre-authorization by the project manager and should be noted as an exception in weekly timesheet reports. Unapproved overtime efforts may require timesheet corrections.

3) Planned resources occasionally record hours before or after their forecast start and end dates. Usually, this indicates that the resource has started early or been extended. The manager would need to update the forecast to capture these adjustments. Occasionally, the resource should not be charging to the project and the time must be reversed.

4) Identify late timesheet submissions and follow up with resources to ensure hours are submitted for the next reporting period.

5) Identify unapproved timesheets and follow up with the applicable supervisors.

6) When resource efforts vary significantly from the forecast or budget, it indicates there is a potential issue with the position. This anomaly requires a discussion on the resource's performance and a review of forecast information.

7) If a resource has entered time against an unexpected or incorrect task, this must be identified, and a correction will be required.

8) Certain types of time are not authorized for project costing. These guidelines are typically related to accounting standards and outlined by the organization. When encountered, the associated entries must be removed from the project.

9) From time to time, an inquiry into the source data is required. These are special exceptions that are not normally resolved quickly. Examples would include . . .

- a single date that has multiple identical entries in the same task code, or
- the total hours reported for a single day are negative.

The identification of these exceptions requires in-depth analysis. Resolution normally involves longer timeframes and multi-disciplinary team efforts. Variances from these issues are managed within the accrual until the problem is resolved.

F. TIMESHEET REPORTS

Timesheet reports should be easy for a project manager to read. As the report should be reviewed and approved weekly, the data should be focused on critical time information.

Costs are a function of the hours and do not require weekly verification. Approvals are more efficient if the timesheet report is not complicated. The cost implications can be discussed during the monthly touchpoint.

1. Simple Timesheet Report

At a minimum, timesheet reports should list total hours by week for each resource on the project. Hours subject to further review should be highlighted for identification. This practice allows the project manager to recognize immediate areas of concern.

	21-May	28-May	4-Jun	11-Jun	18-Jun	25-Jun	Total
Resource 1	24.00	28.00	37.00	**46.00**	47.00	45.00	**227.00**
Resource 2	39.00	30.00	**44.50**	29.00	31.00	36.00	**209.50**
Resource 3	25.00	25.00	24.00	33.00	28.25	30.00	**165.25**
Resource 4	26.00	37.00	36.00	38.00	45.00	41.00	**223.00**
Resource 5	41.00	**(6.00)**	29.00	34.00	41.00	**1.00**	**140.00**
Resource 6	41.00	42.00	46.00	32.00	**72.00**	**84.00**	**317.00**
Total	**196.00**	**156.00**	**216.50**	**212.00**	**264.25**	**237.00**	**1,281.75**

Figure 8-4: Simple timesheet report

A report of this format would be most appropriate for short-term projects with few resources.

2. Advanced Timesheet Report

Advanced timesheet reports can be set up for all labour projects. These documents provide the project manager with enhanced performance information.

In this type of report, the timesheet details would be provided as supplementary information, but the focus is on summary data including additional project metrics. These summarizations enable project managers to quickly identify variances from the budget or forecast.

Additional fields that are included in the advanced timesheet report are . . .

- Budget or forecast hours and variance – This enables the project manager to quickly identify variations from planned efforts.
- Hours submitted in the current week – This summary shows the number of hours submitted by each resource. It is used to identify those that have not prepared timesheets or have entered multiple weeks in the current report period.
- Exception reporting – This identifies hours that may not be eligible for project costing. This could include vacation time, training, general holidays, or unapproved overtime.

Resource Name	Position	Actual Hours	Forecast Hours	Variance	Submitted Hours (This Week)	Exceptions
Employees - Canada		**1,937.00**	**1,937.00**	-	**54.00**	**4.00**
Stone, Arianna	Project Manager	525.00	525.00	-	22.00	-
Stone, Arianna	Project Manager	-	-	-	-	-
Doe, John	Project Admin	199.00	199.00	-	32.00	4.00
Vacant - Project Controller	Project Controller	-	-	-	-	-
Penny, Henny	Project Controller	-	-	-	-	-
Pie, Meg	Data Manager	594.00	594.00	-	-	-
Dough, Jane	Analyst 1	619.00	619.00	-	-	-
Vacant - Change Mgmt Manager	Change Mgmt Manager	-	-	-	-	-
Employees – USA		**3,079.00**	**3,088.00**	**9.00**	**69.00**	**8.00**
Doe, John	Project Admin	771.00	771.00	-	37.00	8.00
Hannigan, Carol	Analyst 2	764.00	764.00	-	8.00	-
Shine, Son	Integration Manager	368.00	368.00	-	17.00	-
Shine, Son	Integration Manager	389.00	389.00	-	(8.00)	-
Tree, Lester	Analyst 2	787.00	796.00	9.00	15.00	-
Contractors		**2,004.00**	**2,014.00**	**10.00**	**48.00**	**12.00**
Penny, Henny	Project Controller	547.00	557.00	10.00	-	-
Bean, Joe	Analyst 1	870.00	870.00	-	38.00	12.00
Bean, Joe	Analyst 1	-	-	-	-	-
Truckman, Blake	Security Resource	587.00	587.00	-	10.00	-
TOTAL		**7,020.00**	**7,039.00**	**19.00**	**171.00**	**24.00**

Figure 8-5: Advanced timesheet report

G. TIMESHEET APPROVALS

After a resource enters hours into the timesheet system, the information is routed to the supervisor for approval. In an ideal world, the supervisor reviews and confirms the total project hours and task information prior to approving the time. This would ensure errors are caught before timesheets are processed.

However, unless solely dedicated to the project, resources typically report to an external supervisor. Further, these individuals could be working on multiple projects under many managers. As a result, the direct supervisor becomes an agent of the project manager, approving hours on their behalf. In turn, the project manager becomes responsible for the externally approved hours.

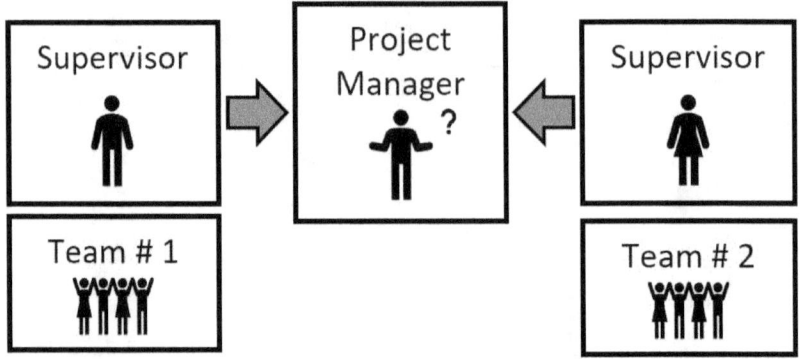

Figure 8-6: Timesheet approval data flow

Organizationally, obtaining the direct supervisor's approval is the most efficient way to process timesheets. However, the project level reporting become subject to errors for the following reasons:

- External supervisors may not be familiar with the project coding requirements, and therefore not able to confirm the accuracy of the entry.
- External supervisors may not be paying close attention to the activities of their team. This makes it harder for them to verify the actual hours recorded.
- Occasionally, large programs are used as time entry "dumping grounds." In these situations, resource time is charged to the project, even if not worked, and the expectation is that over-allocated efforts will not be caught.

The project timesheet process gives the project manager the opportunity to review delivery hours and provide an internal approval. This mechanism enables the direct assumption of responsibility for hours and allows for the confirmation of any efforts approved by external supervisors.

With advanced reporting, the project manager would provide an approval and detailed follow-up instructions each week.

H. TIMESHEET-TO-COST RELATIONSHIP

Although standard practice is to have project managers verify costs, it is more efficient to have them validate hours. The managers agree to a rate when a resource is hired, promoted, or a raise is given. As the labour cost is a function of the hours, the requirement to validate costs is redundant.

The concept behind timesheets and labour costs is basic. Hours are allocated to project efforts based on the entry of the labour resource. These periodic hours are multiplied by the approved rate, and a total cost is calculated.

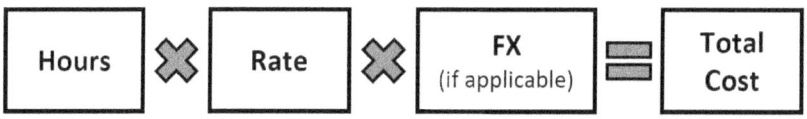

Figure 8-7: Labour cost calculation

1) Hours are the self-declared effort the labour resource has spent on the project. A supervisor approves these hours before they are processed into the initiative.

2) The rate is pre-determined for each resource. Many are standardized by the organization or through contracts. Normally, rates are subject to change at fiscal year end or on contract renewal dates.

3) If the resource originates from outside the reporting country, a foreign exchange factor is applied to convert funds into the reporting currency. Foreign exchange forecasts and conversions need to be aligned with accounting guidance and corporate policies.

There should be separate hours allocations and cost calculations for each forecasted labour line item.

I. UPGRADES OR SYSTEM CHANGES

It is important to note that as businesses and technologies evolve, source system changes are expected. These changes may be simple updates to existing systems, system upgrades, or the implementation of a new system.

Simple updates do not normally impact the source data for timesheets. Exceptions exist if the structure is changed for reports that are provided via manual download.

Prior detailed source data may become unavailable in the event of an upgrade or new system implementation. It is critical to identify project requirements as part of the change process and ensure proposed updates will not impact existing reporting. This is important to complex or longer-term programs, and often ignored. Historic data is either archived or transferred as the total value at transition date. This means detail is either lost or can no longer be matched to the period in which it first applied. Preferably, a "store location" for the past data would be created so that matching auditable records are maintained.

9. VENDOR, SUPPLIES, AND MATERIAL COSTS

This section covers assumptions and reporting related to external supply contracts. These contracts can be for a variety of items. Services, materials, supplies, hardware, or software all immediately come to mind when thinking of external project agreements.

From a budgeting perspective, it is normal to see these types of costs estimated and allocated throughout the project lifecycle. Initial allocation methods could favour a straight-line basis, but S-curve and bell curve distribution are also used. These estimates are expected to be refined during the project planning or design stage. As the vision becomes clearer, it is easier to define the costs. I have prepared initial estimates for road construction based on a single line drawn on a napkin. These values were intentionally overstated, but as the design emerged, detailed requirements were clarified and defined estimates could be prepared.

While it is possible to sole-source a vendor, most contract costs are subject to a tender or bid process. This may occur during the budgeting phase or after project approval has been received. If the selection process has been completed prior to budget approval, the final contract should be reflected in assumptions. If awarded after approval, the estimate can be reflected as an interim forecast update, and a formal change order should be prepared when the agreement is signed.

When the contracting process is finalized, it is important for the project controller to understand the terms and conditions of the agreement. To appropriately manage and model each arrangement, the project controller needs to be familiar with contract terms, including the . . .

- type of contract,
- invoicing amounts and estimated timing,
- payment terms,
- location of supply,
- annual escalation allowances,
- contract cancellation obligations,
- change order rates, and
- earned value implications.

This information is required to properly prepare the forecast and explain variances between project estimates and the final agreement.

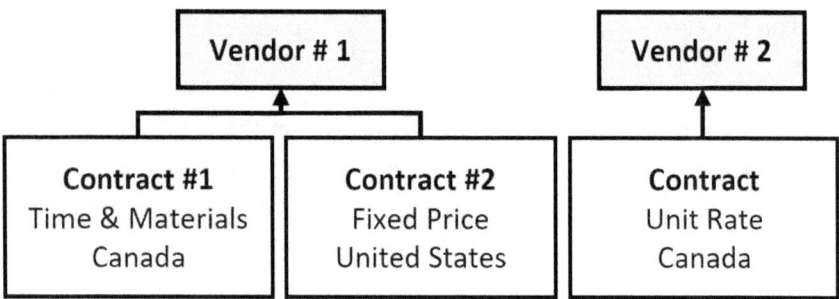

Figure 9-1: Vendor reporting structure

Suppliers vary on a project, and some may even be awarded multiple contracts. To control data and respect privacy surrounding terms and conditions, it is normal to prepare a model to support the separate agreements. These models usually contain detailed information on the following:

- The budget assumptions and timing.
- Approved and proposed change orders, including those relating to contract execution.
- Current unit, cost, and timing assumptions.

Like the labour process, the actual section for external contracts reflects the accrued cost and may include timing or foreign exchange variances when compared to the forecast.

The supporting models may also carry supplemental calculations for earned value or termination clauses.

The agreement also needs to be evaluated within the applicable business processes of the organization. The company may require the contract be captured by supply chain management in a purchase order system. Alternatively, purchase orders may not be required, and the invoices may only need to flow through the normal accounts payable process. Maybe the contract provides for services from different geographic locations, and invoicing will need to be split between the service areas. These process considerations must be understood to effectively manage the approval and payment of invoices.

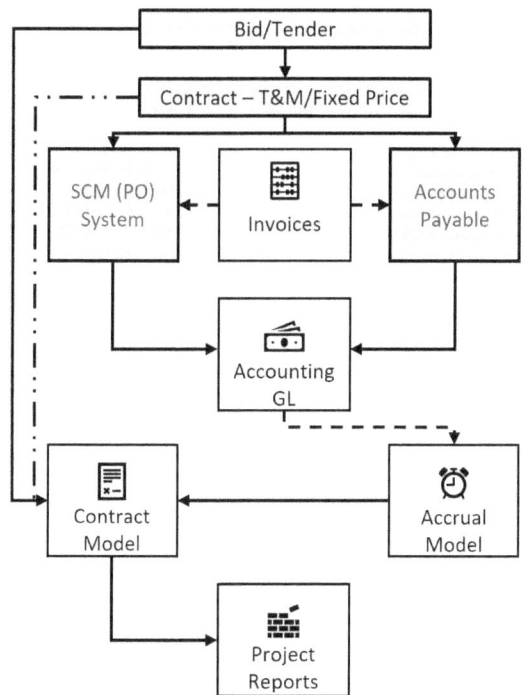

Figure 9-2: Contract reporting relationships

Where appropriate, monthly update meetings for each of these external contracts should be conducted. In addition to the project manager and controller, the supplier representative would be required to attend. Again, the purpose would be to review forecasts and incurred costs to solidify assumptions ahead of month end accrual and project update deadlines.

The involvement of the external team in these regular reviews adds to project expenses. As external labour is typically more expensive than internal efforts, managing the frequency of reporting cycles could reduce the associated expenditures.

The sections in this chapter will discuss specific considerations related to major contractual arrangements.

A. PRODUCT PURCHASES

These are the easiest external contracts to manage. In many cases, these are one-time expenditures and are tied to existing purchase orders. Modeling these agreements simply consists of ensuring the correct price and timing has been forecast. The total purchase agreement must be matched to the original budget item for variance calculation.

Some agreements are more complex. For example, software licensing usually involves an initial annual payment and renewal terms. The controller must ensure that the entire contract is reflected over the project lifecycle. To manage these expenditures from a financial perspective, lump sum costs should be allocated to the agreement terms and not captured as individual payments. There is a timing difference between the cash outflow and project costs (prepaid process). Figure 9-3 shows how the expense recognition differs between the lump sum and prepaid approaches.

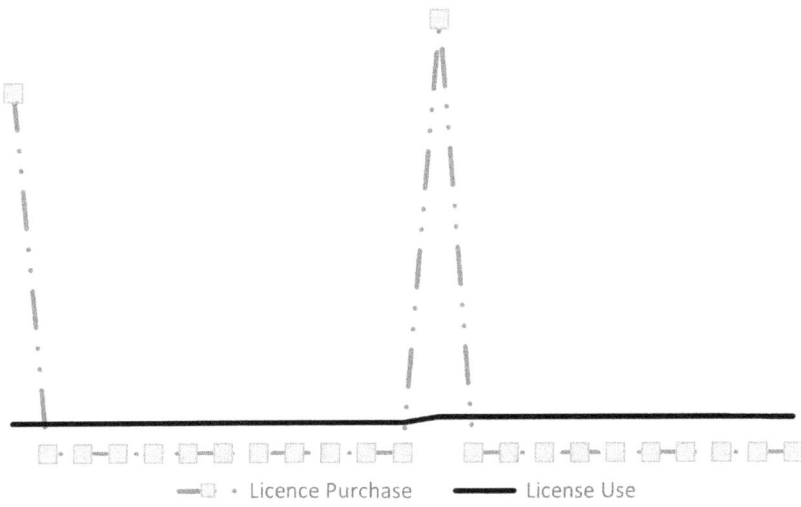

—☐ · Licence Purchase　　━━━ License Use

Figure 9-3: Cash outflows versus prepaid allocations for a license purchase

If the agreement extends beyond the end of the project, the controller needs to work with the appropriate operating department to ensure future obligations are included in budgets. These commitments would include contract terms relating to ongoing maintenance fees, support costs, carrying charges, and transaction fees.

Agreements may also contain savings related to other products used by the organization. Here, the reduction would be reflected in the impacted operating unit, but the savings from the negotiations may be tied to project performance. Coordination must be undertaken to ensure that the benefit is recognized appropriately within the organization.

These one-time agreements could be monitored in separate models or, alternatively, only reflected in the consolidated reporting.

B. QUANTITY-BASED CONTRACTS

There are many forms of contracts that can be considered quantity-based. For this section, I want to address specific issues in contracts for construction.

Construction contracts and project reporting are managed differently than services, and I do not want to get too far into the details here. For this discussion, the periodic allocation of costs will be ignored. We can assume timing expectations align with the approved construction schedule. Further, we will assume design differences are captured and reported through the change order process.

What will be addressed is the management of variances between construction drawings and as-built measurements. As implied, these variances are normal course adjustments between the paper drawing and the real-life measurements that payment is based on. From a construction perspective, invoicing is issued and paid based on the as-built information.

If tracking the delivery at a detailed level, reporting actuals only based on as-built measurements can produce errors in cost-to-complete calculations and impact financing activities. In my career, I found it helpful to project owners, and their financial support teams, if these variances were explained as budget offsets or quantity transfers.

For example, a 150-metre section of underground pipe is designed at an installed depth of three to four metres. When the bid is submitted and the contract finalized, the cost has been forecast based on the approved drawing. Fast forward a few months, and we are now reviewing the invoicing for that section of pipe. The as-built shows the same 150-metre section of pipe has been installed at a depth of *four* to *five* metres, and the contractor has billed accordingly. From a forecast perspective, the original quantity and cost are reflected as outstanding work. The installed product appears as an overage. This would be an incorrect representation. In this situation, there is a cost increase, but it is limited to the pricing difference relating to the depth of the pipe. There is no impact to the total material quantity.

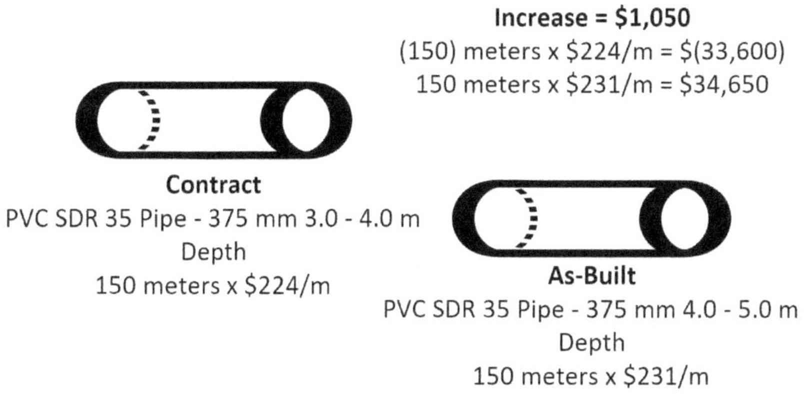

Increase = $1,050
(150) meters x $224/m = $(33,600)
150 meters x $231/m = $34,650

Contract
PVC SDR 35 Pipe - 375 mm 3.0 - 4.0 m
Depth
150 meters x $224/m

As-Built
PVC SDR 35 Pipe - 375 mm 4.0 - 5.0 m
Depth
150 meters x $231/m

Figure 9-4: Contract versus as-built measurement variance

Although the example uses a section of pipe, the same principal applies to surface areas, material changes, and many other reporting items.

A related topic is dirt management. Here, it is not unusual to see allowances for efforts relating to stockpiling, undercuts, or rock excavation. These amounts are included outside of normal contingency calculations. As related change orders are issued, these allowances should be reduced accordingly. When the dirt program is complete, any outstanding forecast amounts should be removed.

Managing construction contracts in this manner was not the norm when I first started out. As a result, some of the managers were frustrated with this approach. However, this tiny process adjustment made an enormous difference to the external funding representatives. They had increased confidence in our team and reporting, as we demonstrated we understood the project and were managing the costs.

Again, monthly change order processing for these variances could be time- and cost-prohibitive. However, these deviations should be tracked and eventually recognized through the standard change process.

C. TIME-BASED LABOUR CONTRACTS

These are labour-based external contracts and are normally related to the provision of services. Agreements based on hourly efforts do not limit total contract value in the same way as a fixed-fee arrangement. As such, they can be viewed by an organization as high-risk. However, they provide the project management team with greater insight into actual vendor efforts. Project managers can use external timesheet reports to evaluate performance and confirm invoicing. This includes the identification of staffing gaps or tying resource hours to expected delivery efforts. Analysis of the vendor data can assist in early detection of delivery issues.

Project reporting for this type of contract would reflect the style used to track internal team efforts. As these processes have been covered in earlier chapters, the information will not be repeated. Instead, we will focus on the differences in the approach to the external reporting:

- Hours for resource budgets and actuals are provided as values. This requires regular data entry and reconciliation to ensure internal project and vendor records are aligned.
- If applicable, the foreign exchange rate on incurred costs is tied to the date the invoice is paid. The rate for each vendor invoice will need to be identified separately.
- In addition to the labour costs, there may be a travel expense component that needs to be managed.

As with internal labour teams, it is expected that run rate variances will occur in this type of arrangement. Part of the variance will be attributable to timing; however, a portion will be permanent. The project owner would want to formally recognize permanent cost savings at the earliest date. Vendors are generally reluctant to adjust budgets and argue to keep the contract estimate whole until the end of project. Detailed project reporting that ties actuals and estimates to timelines and deliverables will assist in these negotiations.

Here again, headcount and FTE calculations can be of immense value for tracking vendor labour efficiencies.

D. FIXED-PRICE CONTRACTS

The final form of contract that will be discussed is the fixed-price agreement. In this type of arrangement, the total value is pre-determined based on the contractual assumptions. Invoicing is normally tied to defined milestones or progress payments. The fixed price typically includes coverage for product delivery and an agreed upon contingency allowance. Travel, if applicable, may also be included, but could be carried as an additional cost.

This is a popular arrangement because costs and timing of payments are predictable and easy to manage. Further, financial risks are assumed to be transferred to the supplier and minimized for the project owner. However, as detailed information is not shared, project managers must rely on the vendor's statements regarding team composition and delivery status. If variances between staffing estimates or schedules do exist, the project management team may not be able to implement mitigation efforts in a timely manner.

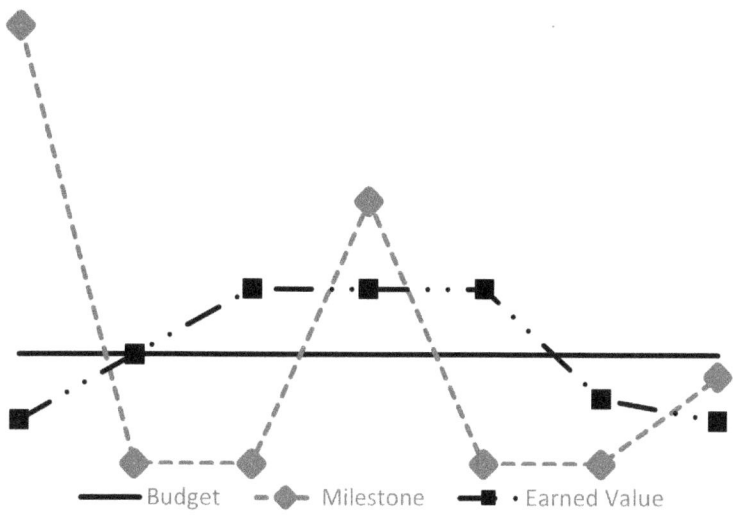

Figure 9-5: Milestone versus earned value run rate

Under a fixed-fee agreement, milestone payments may not apply to every period. Before preparing the contract model, business processes and requirements should be reviewed to determine if there is a preferred forecasting approach. If not, the project manager and controller need to agree on the methodology. These contract models can be based on the fixed-payment fee schedule or on the periodic earned value amounts.

When the forecast is based on the contractual payment terms, it is easy to understand the value and timing of the payments. As the forecast reflects the expected invoicing, no adjustments would be required for cash flow calculations. However, as shown in Figure 9-5, this approach creates large peaks and is not representative of efforts being expended in each period. Further, when forecasting based on fixed pricing, small invoicing delays could change quarterly or annual estimates by millions. I have witnessed these events result in project teams suffering greatly from a minor change in invoicing dates. These teams were penalized in performance and delivery reviews because of a cost timing variance of a couple of weeks, even though the overall earned value was not materially affected. Milestone implications can extend outside of the project, and it is important the organization understands that cost is not the only determining factor for performance.

An earned value reporting approach is frequently used in conjunction with fixed-priced contracts. When incorporating this component, the earned value calculation remains separate within the contractual reporting. The milestone payments and net adjustment to earned value are shown as individual line items. This structure allows for matching of invoices to contract terms and purchase orders as required. Variances between amounts paid and earned value in any given period are easy to identify.

E. EARNED VALUE

Earned value assigns efforts and costs to periods for the purposes of tracking progress against a project plan. This discussion will be simplified to focus specifically on the allocation as it applies to accounting concepts such as accrual calculation and cash flow. Schedule variance and performance index considerations will be ignored. For those interested in learning more, both the PMI and AACE have additional material.

From a controller's perspective, earned value is used for tracking project costs and is tied to determining the periodic value of work completed for fixed-price contracts. These calculations can be completed either on an overall contract basis or by individual milestone.

Earned value cost concepts that are used most often in the financial aspects of reporting are . . .

- Cost variance (CV) = Earned Value - Actual Costs
- Cost Performance Index (CPI) = Earned Value / Actual Costs
- Estimate at Completion = Budget / CPI

These items are used primarily to identify large variances and as a reasonability check for current forecasts. The cost variance is captured as a forecast line item and used to offset the milestone payment schedule. The result is that the monthly forecast reflects the earned value attributed to the period.

	M6	M7	M8	M9	M10	Total
EV Cost Variance	$ (400,000)	$ 150,000	$ 225,000	$ (75,000)	$ 100,000	$ -
Milestone payments	$ 500,000	$ -	$ -	$ 300,000	$ 100,000	$ 900,000
Periodic Forecast	$ 100,000	$ 150,000	$ 225,000	$ 225,000	$ 200,000	

Figure 9-6: Earned value impact to forecast

The format for the earned value calculation should be owned at a corporate level. This will ensure all projects are using the same approach and increase reporting consistency. If the organization does not have a process, the project manager and controller should agree upon the approach and apply it to all contracts in the initiative. This will ensure reporting activities and formats at a project level are consistent.

It is the responsibility of the supplier to provide the periodic earned value percentages for forecasting purposes. The vendor will also be required to provide updates to the estimates as part of the regular review process. The calculation may be completed by the project controller, but both the supplier and project manager should sign off on the earned value forecasts during the month-end review.

If a vendor is reluctant to provide updated estimates, it could be an indicator of potential delivery issues. The manager would need to determine if follow-up is required.

F. CONTRACT CHANGE ORDERS

Contract change orders have been mentioned in the preceding sections. The following discussion will provide additional context.

Like labour change orders, smaller increases or decreases can be compiled and formalized at a predetermined time. Larger modifications will need to be documented and evaluated as soon as possible. All change orders must be approved within the company's financial authority framework.

The following types of contract adjustments should be included:

- design or scope changes,
- quantity changes,
- product changes or substitutions,
- rate changes,
- staffing changes,
- schedule changes, and
- changes to earned value estimates.

As contract modifications could affect other costs, they must also be evaluated to determine the impact to the project. Unlike internal labour change orders, these documents are shared with external suppliers. As such, forms will need to be prepared for each contract affected. Internal modifications will need to be captured in a separate change order. For example, changes within one construction contract will impact the original vendor, but can also affect the costs for engineering, architecture, or the delivery management provider. Each of the parties would be issued a stand-alone change order that documents the effect to their individual contracts. Modifications to the overall project contingency or interest calculation would also be formally recognized. In a service arrangement, revisions to the vendor assumptions can also drive changes to the internal team. Understanding the relationship between the project components will ensure that change orders are correctly prepared.

In some service contracts, a scope reduction is approved without a corresponding cost savings. How does this happen? If I am grocery shopping and remove an item from my cart, my bill is lower. Logically, when a service is no longer required, expenses should be reduced. However, this is not always the case. The project management team needs to investigate these change orders. There could be an undisclosed offset elsewhere in the contract, but this should be identified and recorded correctly.

As with the original contract, it is important to accurately document the assumptions and terms of each change order. These are formal modifications to the project, and it is part of the controller's role to ensure that the appropriate due diligence has been undertaken. These records will form part of the audit trail.

10. OTHER PROJECT ELEMENTS

A. INTERNAL TEAM EXPENSES

Expenses for internal team travel, meetings, or similar events are usually managed at a project level and allocated to assets or teams as part of the final unitization. This approach reduces overhead costs pertaining to reviews, reallocations, or corrections. As there are many rules regarding expense eligibility in projects, it is much easier to contain these costs and limit the scope for review. The project controller needs to understand the accounting and organizational policies pertaining to eligible expenses.

Budgets for these costs are normally determined by using either a set allowance per period or a percentage of internal labour costs. As costs are incurred, these are attributed to the period and expense type in both the forecast and the actual reporting. It is important to evaluate the overall allowance as part of the monthly review sessions.

Variances between the budget and actual spending should be applied to the go-forward forecast. This can be done by adding the net unused portion to the next fiscal period. Alternatively, the balance of the total unused funding could be reallocated over the remainder of either the fiscal year or project. As demonstrated in Figure 10-1, the choice in recognition of unspent allowances can result in peaks or valleys in the forecast.

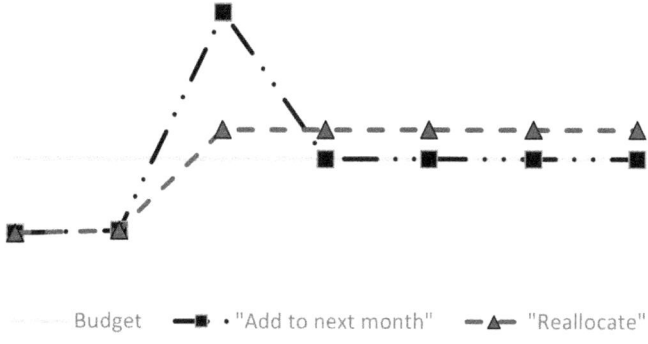

Figure 10-1: Impact of expense reallocation methods

Variances between the budget and the actual spending can also be managed in a separate efficiency line item. Efficiency targets, as discussed in the next section, are a straightforward way to identify over- or underspending.

If the variance between the budget and incurred amounts is significant, the forecast can be adjusted based on the average incurred costs or another approved method. Any permanent changes to the forecast— both increases and decreases—would need to be documented via the change order process.

B. EFFICIENCY TARGETS

Efficiency targets are line items that represent normal course budget variances, both shortfalls and overages. These line items are used to keep the forecast and actual reporting in agreement with the budgeted amounts. As such, efficiency line items represent cost timing variances.

These spending variances are normally tied to the forecast and actual reporting for labour, internal team expenses, and interest costs. Targets may also be calculated for vendor and supply contracts that are being provided on a time and materials basis.

These line items are not used for fixed-price contracts and the associated earned value calculations. Changes to earned value estimates usually involve scope and schedule changes. As such, change order approval is required.

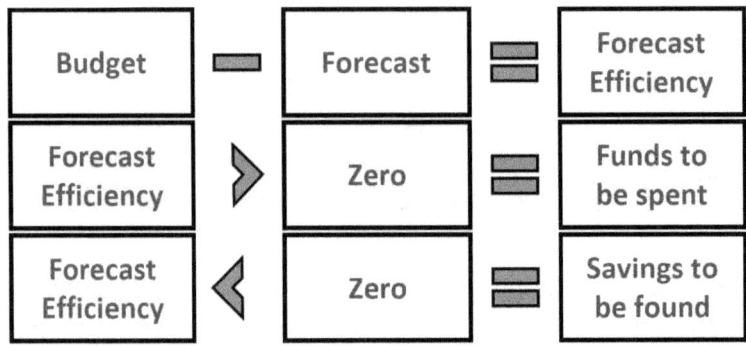

Figure 10-2: Project efficiency summary

Efficiency targets are always calculated as budget less the forecast or actual cost, depending on the specific report. A positive efficiency forecast indicates funds are expected to be spent in future periods. A negative forecast indicates overspending and a requirement to locate savings. As timing variances, these efficiency targets are expected to be resolved during the project lifecycle.

Existing spending variances are discussed as part of the normal monthly review process. If excessively large overages or shortfalls exist, the forecast or budget methodology should be reviewed. These targets become subject to the change order process when . . .

- the forecast assumptions change from the budgeted approach, or
- the efficiency becomes a permanent variance.

In certain circumstances, a timing variance should be carried over a year end. An example of this is accounting for unused vacation time. Here, the run rate reductions for future vacations would be transferred from the current reporting year into the next. This practice moves savings from unused vacations into subsequent project periods. In addition, forecast project hours should be modified to reflect the reduction to expected future efforts. Adjustments relating to timing issues should be formalized as a change order.

C. CONTINGENCY

Contingency is the financial provision for a future event. The value of the event cannot be quantified when the budget is approved, neither can the timing.

Unlike the efficiency targets described earlier, contingency is impacted by permanent project variances. Timing variances should not be managed here. Further, the approval for contingency usage normally rests with the project owner or sponsor. These are not discretionary funds for routine use. The changes require executive approval.

Like vendor contracts, contingency allocations can impact project performance targets. Again, the related financial treatment could affect team compensation.

1. Contingency Timing

When a budget is prepared, contingency is normally assigned to each period based on a percent of the total budget.

If the project is subject to interest, contingency is added before the interest component is evaluated. This practice accounts for the interest that could be incurred by contingent factors on a periodic basis, reducing the likelihood that the budget is understated.

As the project moves from budget into monthly reporting, the total contingency value will not change. The formal allocation of used funds will be subject to the approval and timing of costs under change orders. However, the use of funds does not impact the value of the original contingency approval. The total allowance, RAID reserves, and approved funding changes are managed within a separate report.

Unused periodic contingency should be reallocated to future periods as part of the forecast update process. The cost reallocation depends on the duration of the project and corporate reporting preferences.

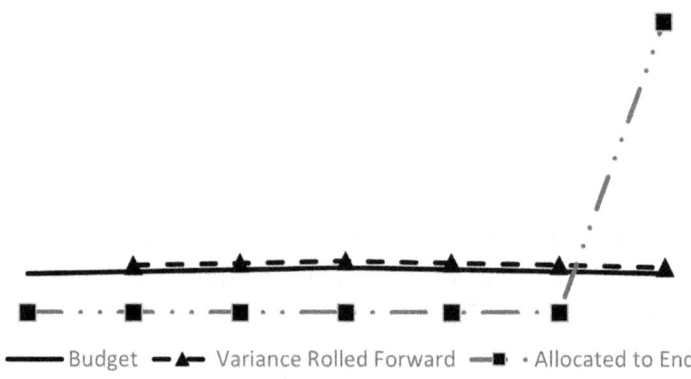

Figure 10-3: Impact of contingency reallocation methods

Figure 10-3 shows the impact of two distinct types of contingency reallocations. In the first, the contingency is applied to the remainder of the project based on the proportionate monthly costs. Under this method, contingency allocations need to be recalculated each month, but the shape of the cost line remains consistent with the budget.

In the second scenario, the contingency has been re-forecasted to the end of the initiative. This approach is not popular as it indicates large outflows at the end of the year or project. However, as the funds remain unspent, the cost will continue to be reattributed to future periods. As a result, the spike could occur as a natural part of normal forecast activities.

In both examples, the total project cost remains the same; however, the distribution of costs changes dramatically. Again, contingency costs would only be formally allocated to forecast periods as change orders are approved.

In multi-year projects, annual unused contingency funds are rolled forward into future periods. This is done to ensure that the total contingency value remains consistent with the budget.

2. Committed Contingency

Funding for proposed project changes that could increase costs should be recognized and reported on a regular basis. This is done by committing contingency funding.

As a reminder, RAID items are the identified risks, actions, issues, and decisions associated with a project. The committed funds are usually tied to RAID items identified as having medium or high probability of occurrence and impact on the project.

When a RAID item is identified, a corresponding cost estimate should be prepared. This calculation should explain the total cost change. The resulting value will then be used to commit or reserve the contingency. If a RAID item is cancelled, the estimate reverts to zero and the reserved contingency is returned to the total allowance.

If a RAID item is determined to be a valid impact to the project and associated efforts move forward, a change order should be issued.

3. Contingency Usage

Contingency is formally recognized as used when it is allocated to project costs via the change order process. As part of this process, estimates should be refined and assigned to project periods. Cash flow and interest implications should also be addressed as part of the cost calculations.

The change order formally reassigns funding from contingency to the project costs. It represents a change to the budget and a new base-line for reporting efforts. Although the expenses are moved into a formal project reporting line item, the associated reduction remains as part of the contingency allowance reconciliation report.

Change orders should never be approved without addressing associated costs. This practice opens the door to undefined project expense increases and arguments between the parties involved.

D. CASH FLOW

Cash flow is different from project cost timing. Project costs should be recognized when an expense is incurred, but there is normally a delay prior to payment. Alternatively, as seen in the earlier licensing discussion, the cost of up-front payments may apply to multiple future periods.

Corporate cash flow is always important to understand and must be included in planning processes. Project estimates can be used to support overall organizational funding calculations. The cash flow can be calculated as part of supporting models but is most appropriately prepared in the consolidated overview.

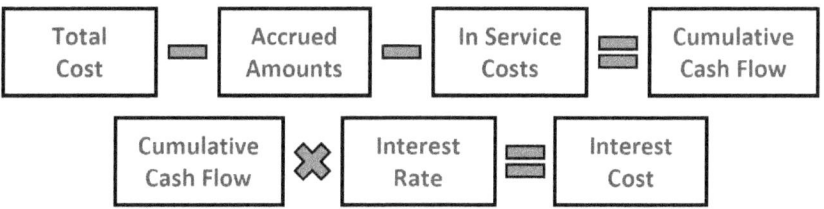

Figure 10-4: Summary cash flow and interest calculations

From a capital project perspective, cash outflows are the basis for calculating program interest charges. The interest rate is applied to the total paid value of project expenses. Committed costs or allowances are excluded from the calculation. As contingency, earned value, and efficiency targets are allowances, they should not be included in total cost-to-date calculations for cash flow purposes. Selling project assets or putting assets into service also reduces the associated cash values and resulting periodic interest charges. Interest is only attributed to the project based on the cash in use at any given time.

As the size of the project increases, so does the impact of using cash flow estimates in interest calculations. Figure 10-5 demonstrates how an accrued amount of 30 percent of monthly project costs can result in a reduction of almost $28,000 to the forecast. As the contingency impact has been ignored in the example, this reduction is solely attributed to the interest.

	M6	M7	M8	M9	Total
Budget					
Opening Cash Flow	$ -	$ 1,109,167	$ 2,227,576	$ 3,355,306	
Project Cost	$ 1,000,000	$ 1,000,000	$ 1,000,000	$ 1,000,000	$ **4,000,000**
Contingency @ 10%	$ 100,000	$ 100,000	$ 100,000	$ 100,000	$ **400,000**
Project Cost - Period	$ 1,100,000	$ 1,100,000	$ 1,100,000	$ 1,100,000	$ 4,400,000
Less Accrual (Net)	$ -	$ -	$ -	$ -	$ -
Current Period Cash Flow	$ 1,100,000	$ 1,100,000	$ 1,100,000	$ 1,100,000	$ 4,400,000
Closing Cash Flow	$ 1,100,000	$ 2,209,167	$ 3,327,576	$ 4,455,306	
Interest @ 10% p.a.	$ 9,167	$ 18,410	$ 27,730	$ 37,128	$ **92,434**
Total Cost	$ **1,109,167**	$ **2,227,576**	$ **3,355,306**	$ **4,492,434**	
Forecast					
Opening Cash Flow	$ -	$ 776,417	$ 1,559,303	$ 2,348,714	
Project Cost	$ 1,000,000	$ 1,000,000	$ 1,000,000	$ 1,000,000	$ **4,000,000**
Contingency @ 10%	$ 100,000	$ 100,000	$ 100,000	$ 100,000	$ **400,000**
Project Cost - Period	$ 1,100,000	$ 1,100,000	$ 1,100,000	$ 1,100,000	$ 4,400,000
Less Accrual (Net)	$ (330,000)	$ (330,000)	$ (330,000)	$ (330,000)	$ **(1,320,000)**
Current Period Cash Flow	$ 770,000	$ 770,000	$ 770,000	$ 770,000	$ 3,080,000
Closing Cash Flow	$ 770,000	$ 1,546,417	$ 2,329,303	$ 3,118,714	
Interest @ 10% p.a.	$ 6,417	$ 12,887	$ 19,411	$ 25,989	$ **64,704**
Total Cost	$ **776,417**	$ **1,559,303**	$ **2,348,714**	$ **3,144,704**	

Figure 10-5: Accrual impact on interest calculations

For minor projects, the impact of cash flow estimates could be immaterial on a project-by-project basis. However, the cumulative effect of this small adjustment on multiple initiatives could be material for the organization. On major programs with longer schedules, using cash flows to support the interest calculation can reduce forecasts by millions each year.

1. LABOUR CASH FLOW

The timing of labour cash flows is dependent on corporate processes. As such, it is important to understand organizational submission, posting, and payment procedures.

The following are examples of the differences between labour cost and cash flow:

- Internal labour project entries are posted weekly. Total monthly labour is accrued. Typically, only 75 percent of the employee costs are cash outflows in the month incurred. The remaining 25 percent is recognized in the next month.
- Contractor invoices are issued monthly, and corporate payment terms are thirty days. The cost is recognized as incurred, but the cash outflow is delayed a month.

2. VENDOR AND SUPPLY CASH FLOW

Cash flows for vendors are also tied to corporate payment terms. Therefore, there is a delay between the recognition of the costs in the project and the outflow of cash.

Project controllers would need to be aware of any special payment terms between the organization and the supplier. These conditions are rare, but when they exist, they impact cash flow considerations and can add overhead costs to the project. These additional administrative expenses would be related to managing the processing and payment of invoices on non-standard terms.

If earned value is being used to calculate the project costs, the vendor cash flow calculation will only reflect the milestone payment. The earned value component does not impact cash.

3. OTHER CASH FLOW ITEMS

Typically, the largest portion of project costs is related to labour, vendors, and supplies or materials.

The next largest cost is the monthly interest allocation, if applicable. This cost is considered an outflow in the month incurred and is immediately added to the ending periodic cash balance.

The remaining costs have little to no impact on the cash flow calculation and related interest considerations. These expenses, including those related to team travel and meetings, can be considered a cash outflow in the month incurred. Exceptions may occur in unusual circumstances. However, the benefit from the adjustment is usually immaterial.

As projects become larger and have longer life cycles, cash flow has a greater impact on the total cost. The proper calculation can significantly reduce interest forecasts for the initiative.

E. INTEREST

In a project environment, interest may be included in the capital cost for the acquisition or construction of new assets. However, the rules and requirements for interest inclusion should be confirmed with corporate accounting and aligned with regional accounting standards.

Normally, interest is managed centrally by the organization. At the end of the month, the interest is charged to the project based on the rate in effect for the period. Rates are shared with the project only for budgeting or forecasting purposes .

Interest rates may be determined based on lending agreements. If there are multiple agreements in place, the interest will need to be calculated and recognized based on the terms of each arrangement.

In larger organizations with a centralized funding structure, it is typical to see a blended interest rate applied to all projects. Individual project components may still have different rates under this structure, depending on the applicable financing arrangements or geographic locations.

Interest rates are subject to change, so they must be confirmed by the project team on a regular basis.

The interest calculation is impacted by the timing of cash flows and the removal of non-cash items. If we revisit the example from Figure 10-5 and reflect contingency use in the final period, the interest estimate is further reduced by $3,500. If the contingency were never used in the project, there would be an additional $2,300 in savings. These calculations are outlined in Figure 10-6.

	M6	M7	M8	M9	Total
Budget					
Cumulative Cash Flow	$ 1,100,000	$ 2,209,167	$ 3,327,576	$ 4,455,306	
Interest @ 10% p.a.	$ 9,167	$ 18,410	$ 27,730	$ 37,128	$ 92,434
Total Cost	$ 1,109,167	$ 2,227,576	$ 3,355,306	$ 4,492,434	
Forecast					
Opening Cash Flow	$ -	$ 705,833	$ 1,417,549	$ 2,135,195	
Project Cost	$ 1,000,000	$ 1,000,000	$ 1,000,000	$ 1,000,000	$ 4,000,000
Contingency @ 10%	$ -	$ -	$ -	$ 400,000	$ 400,000
Project Cost - Period	$ 1,000,000	$ 1,000,000	$ 1,000,000	$ 1,400,000	$ 4,400,000
Less Accrual (Net)	$ (300,000)	$ (300,000)	$ (300,000)	$ (420,000)	$ (1,320,000)
Current Period Cash Flow	$ 700,000	$ 700,000	$ 700,000	$ 980,000	$ 3,080,000
Closing Cash Flow (Contingency M9)	$ 700,000	$ 1,405,833	$ 2,117,549	$ 3,115,195	
Interest @ 10% p.a.	$ 5,833	$ 11,715	$ 17,646	$ 25,960	$ 61,155
Total Cost	$ 705,833	$ 1,417,549	$ 2,135,195	$ 3,141,155	
Closing Cash Flow (No contingency)	$ 700,000	$ 1,405,833	$ 2,117,549	$ 2,715,195	
Interest @ 10% p.a.	$ 5,833	$ 11,715	$ 17,646	$ 22,627	$ 57,821
Total Cost	$ 705,833	$ 1,417,549	$ 2,135,195	$ 2,737,821	

Figure 10-6: Combined contingency and accrual impact on interest calculations

11. PROJECT ACCRUALS

The monthly accrual review meeting is an important touchpoint between the project manager and controller. In preparation for this discussion, the accountant updates cost assumptions, compiles data, and prepares the accrual calculation. Many questions and follow-up activities arise from this exercise alone. During the meeting, the project manager has a chance to review costs and can provide additional clarity on the numbers.

The calculation of the monthly accrual is one of the first things an accountant learns. The concept is straightforward. Calculate every cost you expect to have. Subtract all the costs you do have. The difference is the accrual. Simple. There are adjustments to be considered, but the main concept is not difficult to comprehend.

Normally, the accrual process is simplified at a project level. These instructions generally include accruing for . . .

- outstanding invoices and purchase orders, and
- the labour for a specific period.

When issuing simplified instructions, it is also important to state what should not be included. Some managers accrue interest estimates and unspent contingency funds. This results in the overstatement of monthly project costs.

I have seen attempts to submit proper, detailed accruals. The problem with these attempts was that the entire environment was not considered, and material costs were missed. In one example, all data was being pulled from the accounting system and not matched to source entry systems. In another, locations were missing, and the associated labour cost was not captured at all. The mistakes were discovered when I was asked to reconcile project reporting. In both instances, the errors represented material differences in the cost-to-date.

A. MATERIALITY AND ACCRUAL PROCESSES

The accrual process is an accounting concept. It can be difficult to explain to project managers and administrators that lack a financial background. Further, additional overhead may be required to verify detailed calculations. Alternatively, there could be a negative cost-benefit relationship between the materiality of the accrual and the time required to prepare detailed estimates.

There is an elevated level of confidence in IT systems, so the materiality relating to system errors is deemed to be low. Systems are fantastic, but they are only as good as the assumptions used to build them. Unfortunately, systems are implemented based on the criteria provided by business experts or SMEs. All too often, the SMEs have incredible knowledge within their area, but do not fully consider impacts to other organizational objectives. As an example, I have spent weeks with HR groups trying to resolve project costing issues. Why? Because the HR system development was focused on payroll processing and project considerations were minimal. Even worse, after resolving the issues in one system, the project implications were lost in later implementations.

The other reality is that the larger programs get, the more complex accrual preparation is. It is possible to prepare these detailed accruals, and I have done it throughout my career. However, I automated many of the input processes. Automation skills may not be readily available on project teams and, as such, time constraints may be hard to overcome.

Whatever the reason, the result is that many accrual processes are simplified, and companies accept a margin of error in these calculations.

B. LABOUR ACCRUAL

This section will outline the preparation of a detailed labour accrual from an accounting perspective. Using this method to prepare the calculation provides a monthly estimate on a role-by-role or resource-by-resource basis. The resulting accrual can provide indicators of reporting or system issues.

When reviewing the labour accrual, the following are examples of results that should be flagged for further investigation:

- Excessively large values can indicate timesheets that have not been approved or rate estimates that are too high.
- A negative accrual value can mean rate estimates are low or can indicate duplicate records in the accounting system.
- Task code errors can indicate timesheet coding issues or problems with the backend transaction processing.

Depending on the nature of the role and the number of associated records, accrual variances can indicate minor allocation errors in the project reporting. For example, if a resource forecast changes mid-week and costs are posted weekly, this will result in a negative accrual (overcharge) for one record. This will be offset by an equivalent undercharge on the next record for the same resource.

Foreign exchange rates and timing may also require investigation. These inconsistencies are usually determined following an in-depth review of other error indicators.

Issues like this and those discussed later in this book are not visible using a simplified accrual process. If they are discovered, it could be after years of undetected errors are incurred.

This section will discuss the labour accrual as different blocks of information. Providing the calculation in smaller components will assist in clarifying how the data is related. The example is going to focus on calculating accruals at a resource level. For simplicity, it is going to ignore the additional dimensions of team- or task-level calculations.

1. Calculating Accrued Hours

Figure 11-1: Labour hours calculation

- Timesheet hours – These are the total hours submitted by the resource. If multiple rates apply, hours should be matched to the appropriate periodic rate assumptions.
- Estimated hours – These are the estimated efforts from the last timesheet submission to the end of the accrual period. This calculation can be adjusted for known out-of-office or overtime considerations.
- Total hours – The total hours equal all submitted timesheet hours and the estimated hours to the end of period.

2. Calculating Total Cost

Figure 11-2: Labour cost calculation

- Total hours – These are the total hours, by period, which have been calculated in the prior section.
- Rate – This is the rate in effect for the period, including foreign exchange translation.
- Total cost – The total cost-to-date is the product of the total hours per period and the rate in effect at that time.

Where multiple rates apply, this calculation needs to be completed separately for each period and rate. These costs would be added together to arrive at the total. Estimated hours are normally related to the current rate assumption.

The labour cost each month is fixed at the accrual date and signed off by the project manager. After the approval is received, no changes can be made. As such, it is important to record the date the accrual is prepared. Changes to assumptions or data processed after this will be recognized in future periods.

3. Determining Incurred Cost

Incurred cost is the value attributed to the resource in the accounting general ledger for the project.

It is not always easy to form a direct connection between an incurred cost and the associated resource. As covered earlier, these allocations can be subject to privacy policies. Alternatively, information can be separated into multiple records or expense types. The resource details could be included as part of the description. Determining the incurred value will depend on the configurations between the general ledger and source systems.

Assigning incurred costs to resources is one of the most difficult aspects of preparing the labour accrual. Systems-related issues are further complicated by the requirement to match costs to the timesheet and project records. It has been my experience that the extraction and consolidation of incurred costs is best completed using data automation tools, such as VBA scripts or Power Query. Manually trying to compile and consolidate this information is cost-and time-prohibitive. However, new tools, a determination to understand how costs are reported, and a little ingenuity can overcome that obstacle. Process automation is a wonderful thing!

4. Calculating the Accrual

Figure 11-3: Labour accrual calculation

The last step in the accrual calculation is easy. The total incurred costs are subtracted from the total calculated cost-to-date. The resulting value is the accrued cost. It is this result that can be evaluated to determine if there are any issues in the project reporting or system data.

The total cost-to-date can be subject to change after accrual submission. If the books are closed when the accrual is prepared, there should not be a variance between the total calculated cost and the final accounting value. However, if the books are still open, meaning there are transactions yet to be processed, the accounting cost can change. This is because the incurred cost will change as transactions are posted to the general ledger. Submission deadlines and processes will be discussed briefly in a later section.

C. ACCRUAL FOR VENDOR, SUPPLIES AND MATERIALS, OR OTHER COSTS

The accrual for vendor, suppliers, or materials is easier than the calculation for the internal team.

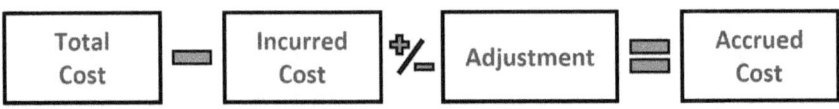

Figure 11-4: Vendor accrual calculation

For external suppliers, the following comments apply to the accrual calculation:

- Total cost – The total cost-to-date can be provided through supplier estimates or from contract documents.
- Incurred cost – This is the total incurred cost per the accounting general ledger.
- Adjustment – These are manual changes to account for considerations outside of the contract value. This could be for a one-off event or for received invoices expected to be paid before the month end.

Description	Total Forecast Cost to Date		Incurred to Date		Calculated Accrual		Adjustments		Total Accrual		Cost to Date (Post Accrual)	Comments
$ 000's												
	A		B		A - B = C		D		C + D = E		A + D	
Contract # 1	$	1,000	$	800	$	200	$	-	$	200	$	1,000	
Earned Value	$	200	$	-	$	200	$	-	$	200	$	200	EV less contract pmts
Contract Payments	$	800	$	800	$	-	$	-	$	-	$	800	
Contract # 2	$	900	$	800	$	100	$	-	$	100	$	900	
Earned Value	$	(300)	$	-	$	(300)	$	-	$	(300)	$	(300)	EV less contract pmts
Invoiced	$	1,200	$	800	$	400	$	-	$	400	$	1,200	Invoice to be received
Purchase Agreement # 1	$	400	$	1,000	$	(600)	$	-	$	(600)	$	400	Invoicing error
Purchase Agreement # 2	$	750	$	750	$	-	$	100	$	100	$	850	PO processing
Travel	$	25	$	25	$	-	$	-	$	-	$	25	
Airfare	$	25	$	25	$	-	$	-	$	-	$	25	
TOTAL	$	3,075	$	3,375	$	(300)	$	100	$	(200)	$	3,175	

Figure 11-5: Supplier accrual report

Important items to remember when preparing this portion of the accrual are . . .

- Earned value is shown on a separate line item than the contract payments. As such, it is possible to have a negative accrual for this record if payment is made in advance of efforts.
- Suppliers may have more than one contract on a project. Invoices must be matched to each contract and incurred costs attributed accordingly.
- Outside of earned value, negative accrual amounts should always be followed up on. These can indicate errors in project assumptions, change order processing, or external allocation processes.
- Adjustments made during the accrual process should be reviewed and incorporated back into the forecast.

  - Adjustments for received invoices that will be paid before the end of the month will not impact the forecast.
  - Adjustments for changes to contract quantities (including earned value) or payment terms should be re-forecasted.

As discussed in the cash flow section, accruals relating to internal team travel and related expenses are normally immaterial to the overall project costs. These items are usually matched to the incurred cost value for the period. Exceptions would only be made in unusual circumstances, such as adjusting for holiday event expenses at year end.

Efficiency targets and contingency are never accrued. These amounts represent undefined spending and do not meet the definition of an accruable amount. As such, they should be reallocated to future periods as part of the month end forecasting activities.

Interest is normally allocated to the project as part of month-end processing activities. It is not included in this calculation.

D. REVIEWING THE ACCRUAL

I cannot overstate the importance of reviewing the accrual each month. Throughout my career, this review has been critical to locating project costing errors.

The accrual is prepared after the monthly forecast review meetings. Therefore, the project controller compiles the financial data and completes the initial evaluation of the costs. This is a review for the reasonability of the total forecast cost-to-date and the proposed accrual value. The accrual calculations would be examined for excessively high or negative amounts. If located, these amounts would be investigated to determine the underlying cause. If the variance can be resolved prior to the month end, the project controller would undertake the action. Otherwise, the anomaly would be documented, and further follow-up scheduled for the next period.

As part of the review, a statistical analysis on the components of the accrual may also be prepared. In normal operations, external supplier costs should be the bulk of the proposed accrual. This is because of the timing delays between invoice receipt and payment terms in most organizations. Project cost allocations for internal labour should be processed regularly, minimizing the accrual value. Statistical analysis provides additional understanding of the total accrual amount.

The project manager is responsible for the financial results, so it is essential this person reviews the accrual before submission. Managers are busy ensuring successful project delivery, so this checkpoint provides them with a final opportunity to convey additional information. This would be the place where the manual accrual adjustments are identified. Further, the pre-submission review allows the project manager to ask questions about overall costs. It also provides a platform for discussing any anomalies that were identified during the initial review. Cost resolution and required supporting activities can be planned.

When the project manager has approved the accrual, it is ready for submission.

E. SUBMITTING THE ACCRUAL

Submission deadlines and formats differ between organizations. These requirements must be identified as part of the business process review undertaken during the project planning phase.

It is important to understand how the submission deadlines are tied to the closing of the books as this can impact the accrual process. If the accrual is submitted prior to month end, costs are still being incurred. Determining the accrual after closing means that additional incurred costs will not impact the calculation; however, this approach requires swift turnaround times as submission is normally required within one day.

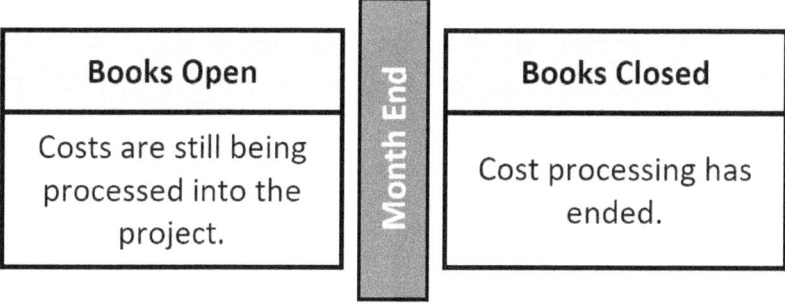

Figure 11-6: Transaction close dates and cost processing timing

It is also important to understand how regional differences impact submission. If multiple locations and accounting systems are within the project structure, it is possible to have different requirements and deadlines by location. Each of these would need to be identified in the project's financial reporting calendar.

If the organization allows for cost processing after the accrual submission, the controller should understand what these costs are, how they are processed, and what impact they would have on accrual calculations. For example, the project prepares and submits a consolidated accrual. Intercompany charges are posted to the reporting project after the accrual deadline. In this case, the project controller can approach the accrual calculation for intercompany activities in three ways:

- Do nothing – Submit the accrual on a consolidated basis and acknowledge that a variance will occur because of the intercompany transaction.
- Remove current intercompany estimates from the consolidated calculation – This would reflect as an adjustment to offset the calculated accrual amount. Intercompany transactions would be posted and recognized as incurred. Estimates for amounts between the accrual preparation date and month end would not be recognized and would become a variance.
- Adjust for amounts to be transferred – This requires the project accountant to adjust the accrual for expected intercompany amounts. The complete consolidation estimate is maintained, and variances are minimized. Differences between the estimated accrual and actual foreign exchange rates could apply.

12. PROJECT REPORTS AND DASHBOARDS

With the supporting workbooks and calculations completed, it is time to pull all the information together into a consolidated view. This will provide the necessary summary information to support project reporting, while the details remain in confidential files.

A. CONSOLIDATED REPORTING STRUCTURE

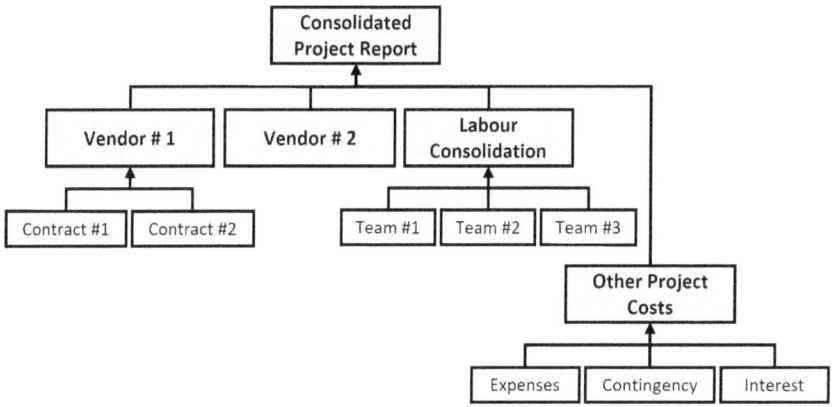

Figure 12-1: Project consolidation elements

The consolidated structure aggregates the information from all supporting models and forms the total cost view of the project. There may be additional cost items that are managed solely within this report. These include expenses that do not require separate detailed support, like team travel and one-time purchases.

It is also common to include the calculations for cash flow and interest in the consolidated report. This is the best place to evaluate the impact and timing of total project costs on both items.

Detailed supporting schedules and calculations will remain in the individual reporting modules. The specific level of data carried into the consolidated view is subject to the discretion of the organization or project manager. However, this information should be sufficient to enable and support overall project variance calculations and the associated reporting.

The consolidated structure should contain summaries for the budget, forecast, and actual results. The total value of the forecast and actual outcomes should be equivalent, with variances only tied to timing differences from the accrual process. Variances can and should be reported between any of these summary schedules. In addition, if multiple budgets do exist, variance analysis will need to be completed for each.

Figure 12-2 is a high-level version of a consolidated forecast. Critical inclusions are . . .

- period identifier, including status as actual (A) or forecast (F),
- schedule timeline,
- FTE and headcount assumptions,
- labour hour assumptions,
- contract information, with a minimum of earned value cost variance and milestone details,
- purchase agreement summaries,
- team travel,
- labour costs and efficiency targets, and
- contingency and interest allocations.

$ 000's	M6 - A	M7 - A	M8 - A	M9 - F	M10 - F	M11 - F	M12 - F	Total
Schedule								
FTE	15	18	20	20	20	10	5	
Headcount	18	22	25	32	32	15	7	
Hours	2,448	2,964	3,371	3,296	3,280	1,552	792	
Forecast								
Contract # 1	$ 50	$ 125	$ 200	$ 200	$ 200	$ 75	$ 50	$ 900
Earned value cost variance	$ (450)	$ 125	$ 200	$ (100)	$ 200	$ 75	$ (50)	$ -
Milestone payments	$ 500	$ -	$ -	$ 300	$ -	$ -	$ 100	$ 900
Contract # 2	$ 75	$ 175	$ 300	$ 325	$ 325	$ 125	$ 75	$ 1,400
Supplier # 1 - Earned Value	$ (175)	$ (175)	$ 300	$ (325)	$ 325	$ 125	$ (75)	$ -
Supplier # 1 - Invoiced	$ 250	$ 350	$ -	$ 650	$ -	$ -	$ 150	$ 1,400
Purchase Agreement # 1	$ -	$ -	$ 400	$ -	$ -	$ -	$ -	$ 400
Purchase Agreement # 2	$ 750	$ -	$ -	$ -	$ -	$ -	$ -	$ 750
Travel	$ 5	$ 8	$ 13	$ 5	$ 5	$ 5	$ 5	$ 45
Airfare	$ 5	$ 8	$ 13	$ -	$ -	$ -	$ -	$ 25
Trave Allowance	$ -	$ -	$ -	$ 5	$ 5	$ 5	$ 5	$ 20
Internal Labour	$ 294	$ 355	$ 404	$ 393	$ 391	$ 184	$ 93	$ 2,115
Employees	$ 168	$ 203	$ 231	$ 226	$ 225	$ 106	$ 54	$ 1,213
Contractors	$ 126	$ 152	$ 173	$ 169	$ 169	$ 80	$ 41	$ 910
Efficiency	$ -	$ -	$ -	$ (2)	$ (2)	$ (2)	$ (2)	$ (8)
Subtotal	$ 1,174	$ 663	$ 1,317	$ 923	$ 921	$ 389	$ 223	$ 5,610
Contingency @ 10%	$ -	$ -	$ -	$ 211	$ 210	$ 89	$ 51	$ 561
Interest @ 5% p.a.	$ 5	$ 8	$ 13	$ 18	$ 23	$ 25	$ 26	$ 116
Total Cost	$ 1,178	$ 671	$ 1,330	$ 1,152	$ 1,154	$ 503	$ 300	$ 6,288

Figure 12-2: Consolidated project report summary

The requirements for variance and KPI reporting will assist in determining the detail that should be carried at a consolidated level. Executives must have access to the appropriate information to enable and support strategic decisions.

B. SUMMARIES AND DASHBOARDS

The world of summaries and dashboards has changed dramatically during my career. The push to clarify messaging, combined with innovative technologies and graphic abilities, has opened a whole new world of reporting. When products like IBM Cognos or Microsoft Power BI are enabled, the possibilities become endless.

There is no need to cover detailed concepts on dashboarding in this book. Training materials and providers are abundant. I encourage prospective project controllers and existing project staff to enroll in a class and let their imaginations run wild.

The requirements for project summaries and dashboards should be set at a corporate level. The data and formulae that drive the reporting should be consistent throughout the organization. This standardization will enable executive management teams to make faster and better decisions across multiple project platforms. In addition, as the data can be pulled directly from systems, the automation of reporting reduces the opportunity for manipulation. However, centralized functions should remain open to suggestions from project teams as new tools continue to emerge and change the way that data can be connected.

There are many templates and guidelines for creating project-level summaries and dashboards. No matter what the format is, these additional items should be kept in mind:

- The audience must be considered when preparing the dashboard. Include instructions to operate the report and do not assume that every user has the same skill level or understanding of the tool.
- Charts and tables should be clearly labeled. Management should be able to understand the information and not have to make assumptions on the results.
- Dashboards should be flexible, even if presented in workbooks. Report dimensions such as time, periodic versus cumulative cost, teams, and display units should be easy to manage and change from the dashboard page.
- If a slicer has been incorporated into the reporting, ensure the settings are correct before copying a chart or summary into a presentation. Failing to clear filters results in cost presentation errors.
- Ensure dashboards are available in the supporting models. These specific views assist in individual team or contract management.

The goal is to guarantee that the data is relevant to the user. Summaries should assist them in understanding the project performance and enable strategic decisions. Meeting the requirements for different management layers may require multiple dashboarding options.

I mentioned earlier in this book that labour has been one of the challenges for project reporting. Figure 12-3 is a sample dashboard that can be prepared using the data relationships described in prior chapters. The first row of information provides quick facts on staffing, including the current period costs, hours, FTE, headcounts, and forecast overage information.

Current Cost	Current Hrs	Current FTE	Current Headcount	Overage to Date	Forecast Overage
$0.17	1,830	13	17	$(0.2)	$0.7

Cumulative Cost

Labour Variance

Resource Management

Filled	Vacant/ Recruiting	Total	Offboard	Onboarding	Offboarding
9	1	10	4	1	10

Figure 12-3: Labour reporting dashboard

The next section focuses on labour cost trends. The waterfall draws attention to the costs associated with schedule delays and new hires. The last section provides an overview on resource management and upcoming activities. This includes information on positions that need to be filled and resources that are leaving.

Based on feedback that I have received, the summary insights outlined in the example have been highly beneficial and focused labour management efforts.

13. EXAMPLES OF ERRORS UNCOVERED THROUGH STRICT CONTROL PROCESSES

Unlike conventional financial models, I have built my project reports to capture a great deal of detail. The reason for this is that the models were not being used to support a single decision, such as a financing or investment opportunity. These models were designed to be a mini "system," built specifically to capture data, reconcile processes, and provide clarity on all aspects of the project performance. The underlying driver has always been the creation of stakeholder value.

Most errors get discovered during the accrual process. It is the time where actual results are first compared to forecast expectations. It is when project managers and controllers can engage in meaningful conversations on performance. Once the errors have been identified, there is still a reconciliation and verification process that needs to be completed. Then, resolution efforts begin.

If organizational controls or business processes are determined to be at risk, it is the responsibility of the project team to report issues for follow-up. Companies should endeavour to investigate the extent and overall materiality of these items. Often the matter is part of a larger data or process issue. More frightening, not all errors are reported. Unfortunately, some managers do not inform the company of process risks and simply make the required adjustment at the project level.

The tables on the following pages provide samples of errors discovered through strong controls and the collaboration of project management talents. The cost of these problems at a project level ranged from $500,000 into the millions. Although many of these issues were identified within projects, there were larger organizational impacts that needed to be addressed.

Inconsistent contractor burden recognition		
Indicator	Issue	Resolution
• Burden accruals were significant (six weeks or more).	• Inconsistent and incomplete contract burden posting.	• Business process re-design, including change to system reporting parameters.
! Issue not reported to organization, as project actuals came in lower and resulted in favourable performance reviews.		

Labour postings missing after system conversion		
Indicator	Issue	Resolution
• Resource-level labour accrual errors.	• Weeks of time either went "missing" or were duplicated in the accounting ledger.	• Organization used the historic project timesheet reporting to assist in locating and correcting batches.

Labour rate errors		
Indicator	Issue	Resolution
• Cross-project rate inconsistencies.	• A single project was using an incorrect annual rate table.	• Rate verification and reconciliation. • Manual adjustment for historic entries and system reconfiguration for future processing.

Missing timesheet information after new system implementation		
Indicator	Issue	Resolution
• Increasing labour accrual values.	• Posting based on date worked, not time submission. • Time corrections not posting correctly. • Incomplete costing.	• Rate verification and reconciliation. • Manual adjustment for past entries. • Business process re-design, including change to system reporting parameters.
!	Issue not reported to organization, as project actuals came in lower and resulted in favourable performance reviews.	

Contractor invoice posting/payment delays		
Indicator	Issue	Resolution
• Resource-level accrual variances.	• Time entries could be completed within a period of one year. • Invoice processing only occurred within a period of three months.	• Reconciliation and special AP process to clear changes outside of the three-month period. • Business process re-design.

Incomplete internal project processes		
Indicator	Issue	Resolution
• Timesheet entries without related cost recognition.	• Centralized project accounting group did not understand the extent of the project environment and systems involved.	• Additional systems had to be mapped and reconciled with the project.
! Impacted project performance metrics, profitability, and inter-company reporting.		

Backend project adjustments		
Indicator	Issue	Resolution
• Task-level accrual variances.	• HR and GL systems not synchronized. • Central accounting group posting errored entries without consulting project staff.	• Manual reconciliation and journal entry posting.

Non-project invoice posted to project		
Indicator	Issue	Resolution
• Negative contract accrual.	• Invoice was not for project but had listed a project PO. • Timing of invoice did not match contract terms. • Invoice approval external to project and based on PO number.	• Meetings between supplier, AP, supply chain, and project to discuss. • Credit note processing. • Vendor refunded company.

Project invoiced for incorrect amount		
Indicator	Issue	Resolution
• Negative contract accrual.	• Vendor billing on pre-contract estimates. • Invoice approval external to project and based on PO number.	• Meetings between supplier, AP, supply chain, and project to discuss. • Credit note processing. • Vendor refunded company for difference.

Accounts payable workflow issues		
Indicator	Issue	Resolution
• Large vendor accrual. • Vendor requests for payment.	• Invoices assigned to resource that had left the company. • Workflow was not reassigned.	• Business process re-design.

Incomplete project billings		
Indicator	Issue	Resolution
• Large, unbilled revenue reports.	• Inexperienced staff. • Minimum revenue targets used to determine monthly invoicing levels.	• Contract reconciliations. • Intensive billing efforts. • Intensive collection activity.
!	Incomplete revenues impacted income statement and cash flow for the company. Collection issues and bad debts related to aging of work prior to billing.	

As the preceding errors demonstrate, strong processes and controls can increase the accuracy of the project financial reporting. They can also validate organizational processes and reduce errors throughout the company.

14. ESG CONSIDERATIONS FOR PROJECTS

Projects represent billions of dollars in spending each year. These initiatives will not be immune from changing political and social attitudes. In fact, major changes for projects may be on the horizon. Planning, estimating, and reporting efforts will be impacted by . . .

- environmental, social, and governance (ESG) reporting and disclosure requirements,
- changing workforce attitudes, and
- advancements in technology.

ESG disclosures are important and intended to drive value in six principal areas. While projects will have to address issues regarding sustainability, reputation, and loyalty, it is the other value-added factors that could have the greater impact. Internal and external stakeholders will expect to see . . .

- greater transparency regarding project estimates and reporting,
- improved risk reporting, and
- increased consideration for the creation of stakeholder value.

The impact of ESG initiatives will be felt by listed corporations worldwide. However, the change will not end there. Companies not mandated to provide disclosures will also need to modify operations. The nature of ESG requires that legislated organizations may also need to include reporting on the activities of both up- and downstream business partners. It is fair to assume that listed companies will be looking for associates to comply with the regulations. If the affiliated companies fail to do so, it will be in the reporting entity's best interest to find new business partners. As such, even smaller companies should be starting to plan for ESG requirements.

As these considerations emerge in the corporate world, projects will undoubtedly face increased scrutiny. Evaluating ESG impacts and including the associated disclosures will become part of the project planning process. It is also feasible that routine variance reporting will become the norm. While there are established structures in certain countries, the full impact of ESG reporting measures is still evolving and being standardized at an international level. Specific project considerations will emerge as organizations continue to adapt to these changes and implement reporting requirements.

Another consideration for projects will be who pays for the additional expenses or fees to support ESG reporting. These costs may relate to specific factors or be limited to supplementary project reporting efforts. The effects will be experienced regardless of whether the project is an internal initiative or an external service. Related charges may be reflected as separate cost items or represent an increase to billing rates.

This chapter will explore potential impacts of changing social trends and ESG requirements on future project efforts.

A. ENVIRONMENTAL

Environmental considerations will influence construction projects. Certainly, environmental impact assessments will play a greater role. It is possible to foresee expanded requirements for this reporting and a more stringent approval process coming into play. However, as the nature of the reporting is changing, and the workload for environmental consultants increases, it is reasonable to expect assessment and compliance costs will rise accordingly.

Depending on the organization's environmental strategy, projects may also be asked to focus on locally sourced materials or labour. This could potentially impact purchasing power or prices. Perhaps the requirement to use local resources will result in higher costs, or maybe the availability of labour will influence timelines. In addition, greater emphasis could be placed on sourcing construction materials from sustainable and renewable sources. Will products like asphalt continue in their current state or will new products be required? How will these source considerations impact project costs and schedules?

In addition to the raw environmental impact, there will be an increased focus on greenhouse gas emissions. Greenhouse gas accounting will require that companies report for direct activities and purchased heating and electrical (Scope 1 and 2). Projects will impact these direct calculations if . . .

- company-owned vehicles or construction equipment are required to complete the project, or
- additional space is required to house project staff (offices or site trailers).

Emerging requirements for the reporting of indirect greenhouse gas emissions (Scope 3) will further complicate project tracking requirements. Some of the more interesting requirements for calculating and reporting upstream emissions are . . .

- The inclusion of GHG emissions for employee commutes. Project teams include augmented staff levels, which will increase the corporate estimates. On top of that increase, this will add an additional layer of data that will need to be captured (method, distance) as well as extra reporting.
- Calculating and reporting GHG implications for team travel. The requirements for project travel can exceed normal corporate expectations. The project team will need to account for the additional emissions. It is possible that travel will require greater justification in the future.

In addition to the reporting, the team may be asked to find ways to reduce environmental concerns relating to the completion of the project.

This discussion provides some considerations for project staff going forward. Environmental concerns will continue to increase in importance as the world moves toward the 2050 net-zero emissions target. As such, both project managers and controllers should seek to increase their knowledge in this area. These individuals should be prepared to answer tough questions.

B. SOCIAL

In my own experience, and in conversations with colleagues, life on a project requires sacrifice. You need to be available on demand and put in whatever hours are necessary to get the job done. Long days and little sleep would sum up my experience. Colleagues are quick to agree that project life is not a nine-to-five experience.

However, strong indicators of change are on the horizon, and project management teams should be preparing now.

The first change is the increasing labour shortage. Baby Boomers are retiring, and there are simply not enough remaining individuals in the workforce to meet demand. Enabling technology could offset a portion of this labour shortage, but the remainder will translate into either increased hours or elongated project schedules. This shortage will have a greater impact on physical construction efforts, as the work required is labour-based and not, at this time, able to be completed via technology.

In 2016, increasing awareness of employee burnout led to revolutionary changes in labour legislation with the creation of France's "right to disconnect" laws. These laws protect the employee's right to personal time and have since been passed in several European countries. The legislation has already expanded into Canada, with Ontario passing a bill in June of 2022 and other provinces proposing similar laws.

Adding to the formal labour recognition, the COVID-19 pandemic changed employee attitudes regarding work-life balance. Many of us had the opportunity to engage with our family, our friends, and our passions again. The pandemic proved that technology had advanced to the point where remote work is possible and alternative work arrangements can be made. However, as the world adjusted to the change in office dynamics, the lines between work and personal lives became blurred. Employees demanded companies respect their non-work hours. Workers re-evaluated their terms of employment and started actively searching for better opportunities. They demanded respect and fair compensation. This change in workplace attitudes led to additional momentum for right-to-disconnect initiatives.

What does this mean for projects going forward? How will changes in the employee mindset, legislation, and protected work-life balance requirements impact project schedules and reporting? First, companies should be seeking greater clarity in labour staffing efforts. As discussed earlier in the book, some labour estimates are prepared based on total compensated hours in a year, assigned to the project on a weekly basis. With employees entitled to time off, this approach is likely to be reformed as ESG requirements and reporting become mandatory. These estimates would need to call out the overtime inclusion and potential penalty allowances for infringing on the employee's non-work hours. Social pressures regarding labour hours and work-life balance could see additional expansions to project schedules. Alternatively, team sizes could increase, along with the associated costs, to enable timely project delivery.

In addition to the number of resources, there is an evolving skills requirement for positions. As technology advances and data becomes more critical in the business world, it is vital that resources have the knowledge and ability to analyse the increased volume of information. From an individual perspective, resources may not be able to afford to upgrade. Maybe they do not have the desire. It could even be that they are not aware of the dramatic change in requirements. Whatever the reason, there appears to be an increasing gap between the talents desired to fill positions and the availability of those skills in labour resources.

The social component of ESG also involves reporting on employment statistics. This may involve a shift from augmenting existing staff with temporary labour to additional permanent hires, or the expansion of external service contracts. Regardless of the strategy, work-life balance requirements still apply to labour efforts and the potential impacts will not change. Choosing to add additional short-term, permanent staff will impact corporate overhead costs and may lead to increased rates on internal projects. Further, if there is not a position in the organization for the resource after project completion, termination statistics could negatively impact the corporate ESG reports. If the decision is to augment staff via an external service provider, there will undoubtedly be an increase to project costs because of the higher external rates.

Another social component that will affect project cost and performance is the passing of modern slavery legislation. These laws have already been implemented in several countries, including the United Kingdom and Canada. Under this legislation, companies must investigate their up- and down-stream supply chains to determine if there is a forced labour component. If so, the company must find an alternate business partner, or face substantial penalties and damage to their reputation. Penalties extend beyond the company – corporate officers and directors can also be held liable under this legislation. When organizations determine that an alternative supplier must be used, how will this impact projects? Will there be short-term delays as vendors are changed, or will these be longer-term if ethical suppliers are suddenly overwhelmed? Increases in the associated costs seem unavoidable as premiums can be expected for "certified" products.

Diversity, equity, and inclusion factors will also impact project staffing decisions. It can be expected that projects will need to pay greater attention to these social factors.

C. GOVERNANCE

The call for better reporting, increased transparency, and higher ethical accountability should trickle down from overall corporate objectives into project governance. With the gross costs of projects worldwide, this seems unavoidable. Evidence of this transition is already popping up on forums such as LinkedIn. Project owners are wondering why it is so difficult to get information on key performance indicators or variances. Service providers are putting together skilled teams to address the issue. With the increased call for governance on spending, enhanced controls and standardization of reporting processes can be expected.

Early in this book, I stated that the role of a controller is not well defined, nor required, in a project environment. Given changing political conditions, is it time to re-examine this role? An accountant's understanding of financial controls and systems, when combined with ethical obligations, places these professionals in a strong position to assist in project governance transformation. This viewpoint is strengthened by the fact that international sustainability standards are part of the International Financial Reporting Standards umbrella. As the sustainability reporting will be part of external disclosures, accountants must be familiar with the requirements.

Spreadsheets are still one of the major tools used in project financial reporting. This is largely due to the flexibility and popularity of these tools. However, organizations will need to increase the governance on this manual reporting. First, companies should develop internal templates and standardize processes for budget preparation, forecasting efforts, and presentation of monthly results. Most projects should follow the standard practice. If unique circumstances exist, project and corporate resources should collaborate to ensure organizational processes and requirements are upheld, even if reporting structures require adjustment. Next, organizations need to address the potential for calculation errors. It is estimated that over 80 percent of spreadsheets contain errors, yet most businesses do not have a formal review or documentation process. Templates should be protected and automated where possible to reduce data input errors. Finally, project reporting and metrics should be automated to standardize outputs and avoid data manipulation.

Perhaps the biggest gamechanger will be artificial intelligence tools. These innovations are sure to streamline and improve all reporting capabilities. However, technology is only as good as the assumptions and data that are used to develop and implement it. The same will be true for AI. As the popularity and flexibility of AI reporting grows, related project jobs will shift further from the reporting functionality to the data analytics responsibilities. I anticipate these roles will fall more towards the younger generations with limited experience and strong technology skills. There is a chance the loss of experienced positions will result in increased reporting risks.

With advances in technology, increased transparency can also be passed on to the organizational executive team. Reporting practices should expand to involve both summary reporting and drill-through capabilities. This type of structure enables executive members to perform their own investigation into project costs. With this ability, executives will be able to obtain increased comfort in project performance.

Continued developments in technology combined with the increasing focus on governance are sure to change the dynamics of project management. Even though direct project labour hours can be expected to decrease, it does not follow that there will be an associated cost reduction. Efforts may be reallocated into data analysis roles. The cost of the supporting platform may exceed the expenses of manual labour. However, a rush to implement technology could also harm reporting efforts, particularly if the associated skill sets make it difficult to find resources, or if the stand up is rushed and background process assumptions are programmed incorrectly.

Technology initiatives are also facing legislative challenges that are adding to schedules and costs. For example, data laws and agreements are extremely important for the protection and safe use of information. Failure to comply with individual agreements or legislation can result

in companies being penalized and facing substantial financial consequences. The role of these agreements in client-vendor relationships,
and associated consequences, is clear. However, these requirements
must be considered even within a single organization. Companies must
ensure that internal data processes and sharing arrangements are com-
pliant with all applicable international standards. Projects are subject
to related cost increases resulting from additional investments in data
security and threat protection.

Risk reporting can be expected to become more stringent in the future.
Although risks are routinely considered in summaries, reporting may
require increased visibility into the potential impacts. Associated cost
considerations, including cost-benefit analyses, may be more predominant in the future. The risks associated with scope and schedule creep
will certainly be subject to deeper review.

Projects may also need to increase reporting and disclosures on value
creation going forward. These benefits could be in the form of synergy
creation, overhead reduction, or reduced processing times. Advantages
are frequently discussed at the beginning and end of a project, but it is
plausible that reporting is going to evolve to require regular updates.
Further, there is likely to be increased scrutiny on any financial benefits
assessed during the planning phase. Projects may even come under
greater pressure to identify additional benefits and justify spending.

Whether you agree or disagree with ESG policies, the reality is that these
legislative changes will influence and shape business on a go-forward
basis. The discussion points covered here are just the beginning. Over
the coming years, the framework will evolve, as will the nature of the
impacts on project financial reporting.

15. CONCLUSION

Here we are on the other side. In the preceding pages, I have shared the major insights gained from my career as a project controller. In summary, those are . . .

- Communication is key. Discussions on cost should be open and occur on a regular basis.
- Data relationships matter. The relationship between systems and the data in published financial reports is imperative to calculating variances.
- Underlying financial assumptions and approaches can have a major impact on project costs.
- Monetary management is more than just compiling project costs. It is a dynamic aspect of project life.

The inclusion of a project controller is a deliberate decision to improve financial reporting and allow the project manager to focus on delivery.

I have dedicated my career to understanding the accounting, the environments, the business drivers, and the systems and processes that come together to ensure successful delivery. I leverage this knowledge to guide project governance but know that I must play my part and rely on a diverse team to get the entire job done.

Perhaps I have not convinced you that there is a valid reason for including a project controller in your reporting structure. At the very least, I hope I have left you contemplating the relationships and decisions that will change the dynamics of project finances. You should be considering if existing processes are providing complete, accurate reporting without impacting project delivery.

As technology, political environments, and social attitudes continue to change, all aspects of business will be altered in dramatic ways. This will include projects. Increased governance and accountability are sure to put pressure on traditional project management practices. Is your organization ready?

ABOUT THE AUTHOR

Alana resides in Calgary, Alberta, and is a dedicated mother to her four children. She spends her weekends with the family exploring the province.

She grew up on an acreage in Carvel, Alberta, and moved to Calgary in 1995. There, she attended the Southern Alberta Institute of Technology, receiving a diploma for Business Administration in Accounting in 1997.

For the next ten years, Alana juggled the responsibilities of single parenthood, building a career, and completing her professional studies. Since then, she has actively sought to provide superior data on which to base project and business decisions. Her goal is to ensure financial resources are employed in a manner that provides the best stakeholder value.

For entertainment, Alana participates in the Financial Modeling World Cup and other global financial modeling events. She believes that these events assist in developing and maintaining critical analysis skills.

www.ingramcontent.com/pod-product-compliance
Lightning Source LLC
Chambersburg PA
CBHW072138170526
45158CB00004BA/1423